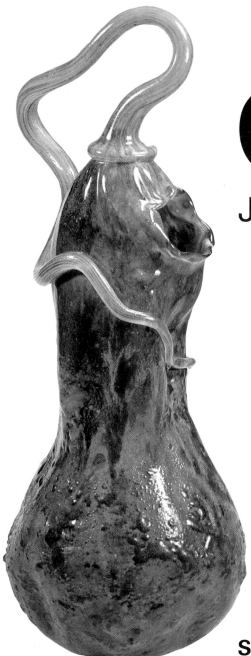

Glass

John A. Brooks

Sampson Low

This edition published 1975 by Sampson Low Berkshire House Queen Street Maidenhead Berkshire

World rights reserved by Western Publishing Company Inc.
Published in 1973 by Golden Press, New York

Created and designed by Trewin Copplestone Publishing Ltd London

Printed in Italy

SBN 562 00009 7

Filmset and reproduced by Photoprint Plates Ltd. Rayleigh, Essex

Acknowledgements

The publishers thank the following for providing facilities for special photography by Geremy Butler: Brierley Hill Museum: 53, 69b, r; Bristol Museum and Art Gallery: 45t, 48, 60, 76, 80; Harveys of Bristol: 46l; Cecil Higgins Art Gallery, Bedford: 38l, 45b, 49, 52t, 56t, 64r; London Museum: 40t, 42, 75t; Stourbridge Glass Museum: 65, 66, 67, 68, 69t, 70, 72t; Alan Tillman Antiques: 73b; Victoria and Albert Museum: 5, 7, 12, 20, 29l, 31, 40, 41, 51, 52b, 56br, 63r, 64l, 73t, 77b.
Other photographs were provided by:
Ashmolean Museum: 21, 44, 47, 57b, 61; City Museum and Art Gallery, Birmingham: 55b; British Museum: 9, 10, 11, 23, 28, 36l, 37, 54, 55t, 62, 72b, 74l and front cover (l); Fitzwilliam Museum, Cambridge: 4b, 14, 36r, 38r, 43; Giraudon: 1, 75b; Tony McGrath/Transworld: 71 and back cover; Metropolitan Museum of Art, New York: 78, 79t; Steuben Glass Company, New York: 79b; Victoria and Albert Museum: 4, 6, 8, 13, 15, 16, 17, 18, 22, 24, 25b, t, 26, 27, 29r, 30, 32, 33, 34l, r, 39, 46l, 50l, r, 56l, 58, 63l, 74r, 77t.

Contents

Page 1 Daum at Nancy was one of the French firms making art glass in the late 19th century. This piece, in the shape of a gourd, is a good example of the naturalistic style popular at the period.

IN all ages craftsmen have endeavoured to produce glass vessels that were both useful and beautiful. Some of those which have survived the centuries to find resting places in the principal museums of the world are unique works of art which can bear comparison with any of man's artistic achievements. Others still exist today in sufficient quantity to enable private collectors to assemble collections which represent the domestic glassware of particular countries or periods. It is the purpose of this book to illustrate these particular aspects of glassmaking from its earliest beginnings to the present day.

The subjects for illustration have been chosen as being typical of their time and place of origin. Some are so important that they appear in many books on the subject, but other items have not been illustrated before and are shown for their relevance to the subject rather than for their rarity.

The various glassmaking areas have been dealt with in approximately the order of importance in which they have arisen, so that the influence of one area upon another may be readily appreciated and make the narrative more or less continuous. This will involve some overlapping of time since glass has been made continuously in several centres over many centuries. It will also be seen how different glassmaking centres have assumed dominant positions in the art, have influenced production in other countries and have then themselves been supplanted by later innovators in the field.

To save unnecessary repetition it will be an advantage to consider briefly the chemistry of glass and to look at the methods of manipulating it. The principal ingredient of glass is silica, which occurs naturally in great abundance in a variety of forms all over the world. Sand, flint and quartz are all sources of silica and if heated to a high enough temperature will melt to form glass. The first atomic explosion at Los Alamos in New Mexico generated enough heat to turn the surface of the desert to glass, and the dark natural glass called obsidian is produced in the course of volcanic eruptions where silica is present. Unfortunately the temperature required (about 1800° C) is higher than could be obtained in primitive wood-fired furnaces, and man-made glass only became a practicable proposition when it was discovered that the addition of a flux in the form of carbonate of soda or potash caused the silica to be melted at a considerably lower temperature (900–1100° C). The fluxes were usually derived from burnt vegetable matter, and in the Mediterranean area carbonate of soda was generally used, while northern Europe favoured potash for its flux. Natural impurities in the silica produced tints in the glass which could be neutralized by the addition of other chemicals such as nitre, manganese or arsenic. This was not a precise science, and the additives often produced tints of their own. This accounts for the wide range of colours to be met with in old glass. Modern methods and precise controls enable glassmakers today to produce a consistently clear and colourless glass. The glass itself is usually referred to as the metal. By the addition of copper, cobalt, iron, tin and other materials, blue, red, green, amber, white or purple glass can be achieved.

At the end of the 17th century, George Ravenscroft added lead oxide to his glass and produced what we now call lead crystal glass, noted for its brilliance, which made English glass supreme for 100 years.

The earliest method of fashioning glass was by moulding. Blowing was discovered during the 1st century BC, but by the end of the 1st century AD virtually every technique for manipulating and decorating glass had been discovered – moulding, free blowing, blowing into a mould, cutting, engraving, enamelling, gilding, overlaying with layers of coloured glass, enclosing the decoration between layers of glass, *millefiori*, and glass made to look like natural stone. All these were practised 2000 years ago and have reappeared at various times down to the present day.

In the same way most of the tools employed in making glass vessels by hand have remained unchanged for many centuries, partly because they are so simple that they allow for little improvement. The principal ones which will be referred to are the blowpipe on which a quantity of molten glass is gathered, and from which the vessel is produced; the pontil iron, a solid metal rod, the end of which is heated and applied to the base of the vessel so that it may be supported when the blowing pipe is cut away (when this rod is removed it leaves the characteristic mark seen on many old vessels known as the pontil mark); and the marver, a flat plate on which the vessel is rolled during the blowing process to smooth it and give it the desired shape. In a glassworks handmade glass is usually produced by a team of three or four men called a chair, and the size of the factory is reckoned by the number of chairs working in it.

Egypt

Below A blown drinking cup with an applied ring handle. The decoration consists of rings of glass applied to the outside and lightly pressed in. It was made in the 8th to 9th centuries BC.

THE earliest glass vessels which can be dated accurately are those discovered in the tombs of ancient Egypt. A small glass jar found in an Egyptian tomb bears the name of King Thothmes III, who lived from about 1504–1450 BC.

Glassmaking, however, must have started considerably earlier than this to have produced such elegant articles by the 15th century before Christ. In any discussions of Egyptian glass, therefore, it is necessary to examine the origins of glassmaking. Current scientific opinion believes that the manufacture of glass originated in western Asia in the region of Mesopotamia some time before 2000 BC, although only fragments dating from this period have so far been discovered. This seems a reasonable supposition, since the Egyptian pieces referred to above exhibit a considerable mastery of the art which must have taken some considerable time to achieve.

This small flask, made in Alexandria in the 1st century AD, is composed of vertical alternate bands of clear glass containing flecks of gold and opaque green glass shot with blue and yellow.

4

Below *A small vase made in Egypt about the 14th century BC. It is made of blue glass with yellow and white combed trailing, and has four applied loop handles in translucent blue glass.*

The earliest glass objects to be found are beads, which were probably fashioned from lumps of glass. As man gradually became more fluent in its manufacture and manipulation he learned to make small vessels of glass to hold oils and perfumes. Tomb paintings dating from about 2000 BC depict men apparently in the act of glass blowing, but as blowing is not thought to have been discovered before the 1st century BC, this must be considered unlikely.

King Thothmes is known to have made expeditions into Asia from 1480 BC onwards, and if glassmaking was not then known in Egypt what is more likely than that he brought home with him glass craftsmen so that he could have glass vessels made in his own country.

It seems likely that the art of glassmaking originated somewhere where there was a closed furnace able to achieve sufficiently high temperatures to fuse the raw materials. A possible place for this to happen would be a pottery kiln, as the potter's craft was already long established when glass first made its appearance, and potters certainly already knew the art of glazing. The transition from using glass for glazing to its becoming a manufacturing material in its own right was probably a slow one. First of all, as already mentioned, rough lumps of glass were cut and ground into beads suitable for making necklaces; then it was found that it could be poured into small open moulds to produce figures of deities, animals and so on. Then finally hollow vessels started to appear. The fact that the glass vessels found in Egypt show a considerable degree of development, and that no evidence has been found of simpler or more primitive vessels lends support to the idea that the art in Egypt started with the advent of skilled craftsmen from some other country.

Small pots and bottles continued to be made with little change until about 1200 BC. Then a period of strife, which lasted for about 300 years, overtook the eastern Mediterranean cultures, and the craft of glassmaking appears to have declined.

However, by 900 BC conditions had improved, and glassmaking started to expand again. The Phoenicians who lived in what is now the Lebanon became the great travellers and traders of the period, and were responsible for the distribution of glass over a wide area, stimulating a demand for it in new markets.

Glassmaking continued in Egypt, and small vessels dating from the 5th–6th century BC have been found which resemble those of an earlier period. It was not until the founding of

Opposite *Egyptian scent flask of green opaque glass formed on a core. The outside has combed trails of white threads. It was made about the 5th century BC.*

Below *An early example of a drinking glass with a stem, made at Alexandria in Egypt between the 5th and the 8th century.*

Alexandria by Alexander the Great in about 330 BC that glassmaking once again started to flourish in Egypt. Alexandria became an important centre of culture and learning, and it would be natural for such a city to attract skilled craftsmen and to provide a suitable climate for developing new styles and techniques. In this way its wares became much in demand throughout the civilized world, and Alexandrian craftsmen carried their skills to other countries such as Greece and Italy.

Until the advent of glass blowing in the 1st century BC, glass vessels were made by one of three methods:

Molten glass applied to a core.
Moulding in closed moulds.
Cutting from the solid.

In the first method a clay core was built up around the end of a rod and covered with molten glass or wound with a drawn thread of glass. This would then be successively rolled on a flat plate and reheated until the desired external profile was achieved. Then when the glass was set the rod could be withdrawn and the clay core chipped or soaked out. An elaboration on this method would be to apply thin threads of glass of a different colour to the outside of the vessel. These could then be combed with a metal tool to form a zigzag pattern and rolled in to produce a patterned surface.

Moulded objects were made either by pouring molten glass into a mould produced by the "lost wax" process, or filling a two-part mould with powdered glass and then firing it. In this way articles like bowls with moulded decoration could be produced. Cutting from the solid was a method by which carved blocks of glass might be treated, in the same way as lumps of rock crystal or other natural minerals.

Alexandria continued as a glassmaking centre for about 1000 years, and during that time it produced a wide range of beautiful and imaginative glassware.

Rome

DURING the 1st century BC two events occurred which were to have a profound effect on the development of glassmaking. They were the introduction of glass blowing and the rise of the Roman Empire.

Nobody knows where or when the ability to blow glass was first discovered, but the earliest datable pieces of blown glass occur in Syria just before the start of the Christian era.

It caught on with remarkable rapidity and within 100 years it had become a highly developed art and had spread to all the Mediterranean centres. This is not surprising since glass blowing offered a cheap and efficient method of producing glass vessels in a variety of new shapes. Blowing into an open mould was a simple way of producing intricate shapes, and free blowing permitted the rapid production of objects such as bowls, dishes and plates which could previously only have been produced in moulds. Considering how conservative and resistant to change was the style of domestic objects generally among the old civilizations, it is remarkable that the possibilities of glass blowing should have been so quickly exploited and used to develop the new shapes that this material permitted.

Up till now the use of glass had largely been confined to a few countries at the eastern end of the Mediterranean, but the colonial aspirations of the Romans were soon to change all that. As previously stated glassmakers had taken their skills to Italy and Rome to satisfy the demand of a rapidly growing Roman state which was, by the beginning of the

Christian era, becoming a sophisticated society whose citizens were acquiring a taste for, and who could afford, the elegant glasswares of Alexandria and Syria. It is probable that in a comparatively short time a considerable manufacturing capacity would develop to supply the demands of the Roman market. Roman pottery was coarse and heavy, and vessels of glass would have been regarded in the same light as good porcelain is today.

As the legions of Rome spread throughout Europe and the Roman way of life was introduced into the countries which are now Germany, France, the Low Countries and Britain, settlers from Rome would arrive bringing with them the familiar objects of their life at home, among which would be glass vessels of all kinds: bottles, jars, jugs, bowls, dishes, plates and so on. It would not be long before the native populations of the conquered countries adopted Roman tastes for these things, and as glass furnaces were easy to set up and it was more convenient to produce the glass where the market existed than to carry it for hundreds of miles over poor roads, a domestic market was created.

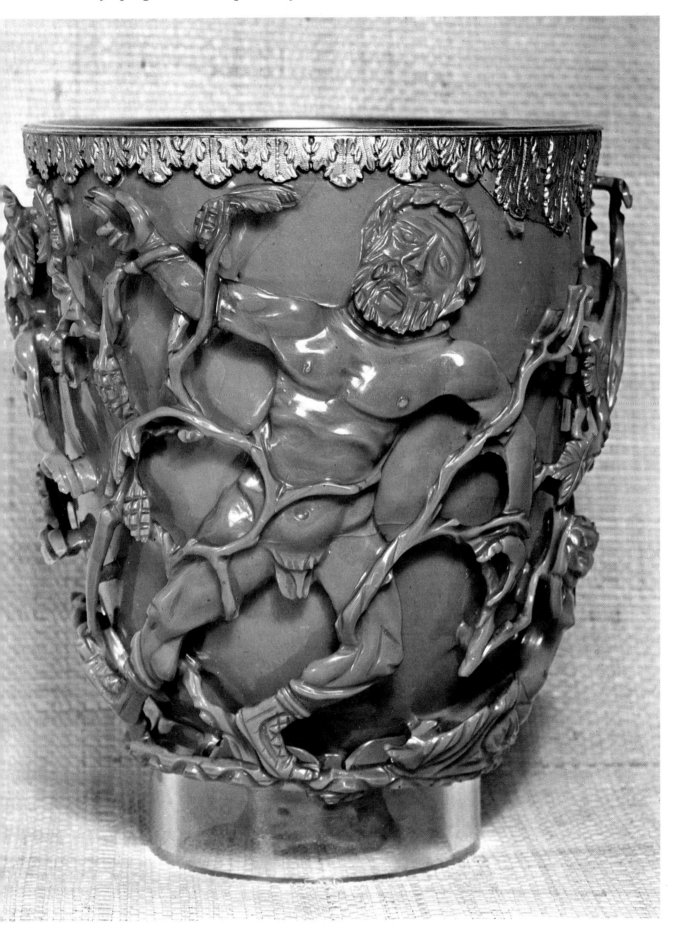

The Lycurgus cup. A carved cup in pea-green glass, the relief decoration of which depicts the death of Lycurgus. Due to the presence of minute quantities of gold, it shines a deep purple in transmitted light. It was made in Rome in the 4th century AD.

A mould-blown Roman flask of the 1st century AD with a long neck over a finely detailed male head. This was found in Cyprus.

The glassworks were set up where supplies of raw materials and fuel were readily available and, initially under guidance from craftsmen imported by the Romans, the familiar objects in the Roman style were produced.

The difficulty now, at this distance in time, is to decide which of the pieces of glassware that have survived to this day are of Italian origin, and which were locally produced. For many years the same styles were current throughout the Roman Empire, and pieces made in identical styles have been found as far apart as England and Syria. It was not until the decline of the Roman empire, when its unifying force was no longer effective, that the various glassmaking centres which it established started to develop the different national characteristics by which we now identify them.

Generally speaking, glass style and production was elaborate and expensive during the first two centuries of the Roman Empire, while it was still a home-based industry. During the following two centuries quality fell while the industry expanded all over Europe and produced a multitude of simple and inexpensive wares to meet a rapidly expanding market, until finally the subject countries started to acquire a degree of sophistication which could only be satisfied by higher-quality styles.

Nonetheless, throughout the whole of this period there were always master craftsmen for whom the only standards were the highest available because there was always a demand for the very best in Rome.

Of the wares themselves the most informative and amusing, although by no means the most impressive, were the blown and moulded bottles and beakers of various types. They range from small scent bottles moulded to represent shells and dates to large bottles with beautifully moulded heads, presumably of deities. They include hexagonal bottles decorated with geometric patterns and beakers moulded with continuous bands showing chariot races or scenes from mythology. A few even carry the name of the maker; among these appear the names ENNION and FRONTINUS.

A speciality of the Roman glassmakers, though one which came originally from Egypt, was the production of *millefiori* vessels. These were made by assembling short lengths of multi-coloured glass canes around a form or core, covering them with a mould and then firing them so that they fused into one mass and adopted the shape of the mould. It is difficult to believe when looking at these that they were made about 2000 years ago.

The "Portland" vase, one of the best-known pieces of glass in the world. The white overlay is cut to show figures against a dark blue background.

Three pieces of Roman glass which are particularly outstanding are the "Portland" vase, the "Lycurgus" cup and a bowl with gilt decoration trapped between two layers of glass. These three items illustrate vividly the heights to which glassmaking can ascend, and also demonstrate that we have not learned anything really new about the manipulation and decoration of glass since they were made.

The fragments of several vessels which have a gold-leaf decoration sealed between layers of glass are known. Most of these date from the early Christian period and have designs of Christian religious significance cut into the gold leaf, but the most remarkable example is a bowl from a tomb at Canosa in Italy. This is a hemispherical bowl about $7\frac{1}{2}$ inches in diameter by $4\frac{1}{2}$ inches high, made in two parts. Each part was cast in a two-piece mould and then ground and polished so that one piece fitted closely over the other. The inner layer had a sheet of gold leaf applied to it, in which was cut a pattern of stylized foliage. The outer layer was then fitted over it, and the edges fused to seal in the decoration. This is a difficult technique which requires the highest skill for its execution.

The Portland vase must be well known to all students of ancient glass, but its history is sufficiently interesting to bear repetition. It is a cameo vase of the late 1st century BC or early 1st century AD, $9\frac{1}{2}$ inches high by about 7 inches wide. The ground colour is dark blue with a casing of white glass which has been cut and carved away to leave a scene from mythology which is commonly taken to represent the legend of Peleus and Thetis. The skill with which the white casing has been reduced in thickness to allow the dark background to show through in varying degrees to give subtleties of shading illustrates the hand of a master artist at work. The vase was first recorded in 1642 as being in the Barberini palace, and was popularly said to have been discovered in a Roman tomb on the Appian Way. It was purchased by Sir William Hamilton for 1000 guineas ($2500) in 1748, and he subsequently sold it to the Duchess of Portland in 1785 for 1800 guineas ($4500). In 1810 it was loaned to the British Museum where it has remained ever since. Josiah Wedgwood, the great English potter, was so impressed by it that he borrowed it to make some copies in the new jasperware that he had recently developed. After four years' work he eventually produced a vase which was an exact copy of the original. A series of forty of these was made, and the most recent one to come on the market in our time brought £20,000 ($50,000) at auction. The original was commonly thought to be made of pottery, although Wedgwood declared that it was glass. This was confirmed in 1845 when it was attacked and smashed in the British Museum. Wedgwood's copy was used as a model for its reconstruction.

John Northcote, a famous glassmaker of Stourbridge, also spent several years attempting to make a glass copy of the vase in the original cameo style during the late 19th century. As it neared completion stresses produced by the differing layers of glass caused it to split. This led Northcote to research the means whereby different layers of glass could be superimposed on one another, and finally led to the development of cased glass from which the beautiful cameo vases of the late 19th century were produced.

The Lycurgus cup, made in Italy during the 4th century AD, is quite unique in both metal and decoration. It is about $6\frac{1}{2}$ inches high and just over 5 inches wide. It is made from a thick-walled blank of glass, which looks pea green in reflected light and a reddish-purple in transmitted light (This is due to the presence of gold in its composition). The wall was then cut and carved away to leave a series of figures in openwork standing clear of the cup, and attached to it only by a series of thin bridges. The figures represent the death of Lycurgus,

Two examples of blown glass, both of the 1st–2nd centuries AD. On the left a round bottle with depressed top and narrow neck. The glass was originally transparent and greenish in colour, but has acquired a surface iridescence due to the passage of years. The beautiful blue jug with an applied opaque white handle on the right demonstrates the knowledge of colouring possessed by the early glassmakers.

and although the foot is missing it is a work of art which cannot fail to make a considerable impact on the viewer. The artist who carved it had a complete mastery over his medium that can rarely have been equalled in the history of glass.

To sum up: all the major glassmaking centres of the world came under the domination or influence of Rome, who in the course of expanding her empire spread the art of glassmaking throughout Europe. Important glass centres grew up, but the glass they produced remained essentially Roman with only minor regional variations until the Empire collapsed. Although we talk of glass being German or Syrian, until about 400 AD it may more accurately be described as Roman.

The Middle East and Islam

REFERENCE has already been made to the early glassmakers of Mesopotamia and Syria in the context of glassmaking throughout the ancient world. We should now consider them in the context of the development of Middle Eastern glass which had its culmination in the distinctive and sophisticated wares of Islam.

The skills of the glassmaker were in demand over a wide area, and as it was probably easier to set up a workshop where the demand existed rather than export the finished product over long distances (we shall see in a later chapter what complications that could produce), they set up their glass pots in such

This fine mosaic bowl of the 1st century AD was made from segments of coloured glass fused together in a mould. This technique, like that used in making millefiori *glass, was a speciality of the Roman craftsmen.*

countries as Cyprus, Greece, Italy and eventually throughout the Roman Empire. Even though they passed on their skills to craftsmen of other nationalities, they so dominated design and method that the styles they created became the universal standard. In this respect the Syrian style, based on blow moulding, made more impact than the Alexandrian, although both tastes can be traced in glasswares throughout the Roman period.

With the decline of Rome and the transfer of the seat of the Roman Empire to Constantinople in 350 AD the capital of the Empire was right on the doorstep of the Syrian glasshouses which were established at Tyre and Sidon. It has been remarked on by many authorities that in spite of its magnificence and importance Constantinople appears never to have had any tradition of glassmaking. I think this can be explained by the fact that since it was so close to Syria, whatever glass was made in the capital followed closely in the Syrian tradition, and it is also probable that there was never any great necessity to set up an independent manufacture when the best glass the old world had to offer was so close at hand.

Glass of this early period is similar to that found throughout the Roman Empire, but during the Sassanian period (about 100 BC to 600 AD) leading up to the advent of Islam a tradition for cut glass grew up. For this purpose the glass needed to be thicker than the earlier blown and moulded styles in order to carry the decoration. Cutting generally took the form of facets or geometric patterns and was developed to a very high standard.

During the 7th century all the countries of the Middle East came under the influence of Islam, and in 634 Damascus was declared its capital. This change in the balance of power affected glass production, which stagnated for a long time until the rise of the Abbasid dynasty and the removal of the capital to Baghdad in Mesopotamia in 750 AD. By this time the whole area had become settled under the rule of Islam and new styles in glass slowly began to emerge to suit the tastes of a new society. Mesopotamia, one of the earliest centres of glassmaking, was now back in business. Baghdad was out of the main stream of an area which had been unsettled for many years, and close to Persia, which had not been affected to the same extent. The decorative arts had been able to flourish in Persia so that her influence became more pronounced in the glass which was then being produced for the whole area under the domination of Islam.

Opposite *A 2nd-century flask of Syrian manufacture with a trailed snake thread pattern.*

Below *A rhyton, blow-moulded in the shape of a boot on a short pedestal base. There is a row of applied looped trailing down the back.*

Below *A 14th-century glass lampshade called a mosque lamp. This would have been suspended from the three loops on its body. It is decorated with quotations from the Koran in blue and white enamels thickly applied.*

Opposite *A Syrian bottle of the 14th century. The transparent brownish glass is covered with an enamelled pattern mainly in red and blue. Round the body the pattern takes the form of texts from the Koran.*

This new era saw the introduction of a wide range of decorative techniques. Cutting was developed to imitate carved rock crystal; surface decoration in applied glass, gilding and enamelling appeared and some cameo glass has been recorded. Probably the pinnacle of achievement in Islamic glassmaking is epitomized by the lampshades, now normally called mosque lamps. They date mostly from the 13th to the 14th centuries, and are fine examples of glass blowing in their own right. Their more particular claim to fame, however, is the enamelled decoration they carry. This is usually heavily laid on in vitreous enamel in an intricate abstract pattern (the Koran forbids representational decoration) interspersed with quotations from the Koran. The enamel was fired to produce brilliant and lasting designs.

In 1258 there was a Mongol invasion of Persia, and following this glass decorated in the Chinese style made its appearance. The glass of the Islamic world went into a decline when the whole of the Middle East was over-run by Tamerlane in 1402; this gave Venice the opportunity to expand and take over the markets which had previously been supplied from the East.

Seine-Rhine

THE decline of the Roman Empire during the late 4th and early 5th centuries left Northern Europe at the mercy of the various tribes which the Romans had for so long held at bay. A period of turmoil followed, but eventually the Franks from the Rhineland became the dominant power, and stability was slowly restored. During the period of strife glassmaking suffered as it had done much earlier during the turbulent period of 1200–900 BC in the Middle East, but with peace a new demand arose for glassware. This time, however, with the Roman influence gone, a regional style emerged which spread throughout the area between the Seine and the Rhine.

The underlying tradition of glassmaking was that of the Syrian glass craftsmen who had prospered under Roman protection. What now appeared was a modification of the earlier style, which is easily discernible if the two periods are compared. The 2nd-century snake-thread vase found in Syria is readily related to a vase of similar style from Cologne made in the 3rd century although the German example has coloured trailing. The claw beakers, to be

17

referred to later, can be seen as direct descendants of the 1st-century beaker from Syria which is mould-blown with a pattern of what may be considered to be rudimentary claws.

The known glassmaking centres at that time were Cologne, Liège, Namur, Amiens and Beauvais. Excavation in England has produced a considerable quantity of examples of glass of the 5th to 7th centuries, and although no firm evidence has been found of its having been made in England, it seems reasonable to assume that growing demand would encourage its manufacture locally.

A point to bear in mind is that with the rise of Christianity the practice of burying the dead with their possessions slowly declined, depriving later investigators of a valuable source of early artefacts. However, this custom did continue in Northern Europe until the beginning of the 8th century, and this accounts for most of the specimens of glass we have.

The vessels themselves fall into several categories. Simple palm cups without handles, so called because they were held in the palm of the hand when used; cone beakers up to 10½ inches high, tapering to a narrow base which were also intended to be held rather than to stand; a variety of squat pots and bottles, and the claw beakers already mentioned. These, although rather ugly to look at, are undoubted masterpieces of glassmanship. The basic shape is rather that of the cone beaker, but further lumps of glass were applied to the outside and then blown and drawn out to resemble rather squat elephants' trunks. The ends were then re-attached to the body of the glass.

The feature of all these glasses which gives them their character is the applied decoration which consists of threads of glass trailed on to the outside in various patterns. The commonest method was to wind a thin thread of glass several times around the upper and lower sections of the vessel at right angles to the height, but vertical trailing was also used. In some instances parallel threads were drawn together at intervals to form a series of diamonds. This fashion was to be revived 1000 years later by Ravenscroft on his "glass of lead".

The metal itself is usually of a greenish colour of varying intensity, which was caused by the materials used, including potash derived from burning wood and vegetable matter, and is referred to as *Waldglas*. It is sometimes supposed that it was beyond the skill of these glassmakers to produce clear glass, but Thorpe in his book *English Glass* expressed the opinion that the green colour was produced from choice.

Opposite *This type of vessel is called a bag pot because of its shape, suggesting a leather pouch. This example, from the Seine/Rhine area, was made during the 6th century.*

An elegant beaker glass from the Rhine district, made in about the 4th century AD. The trailed thread decoration is typical of the glass made in this area.

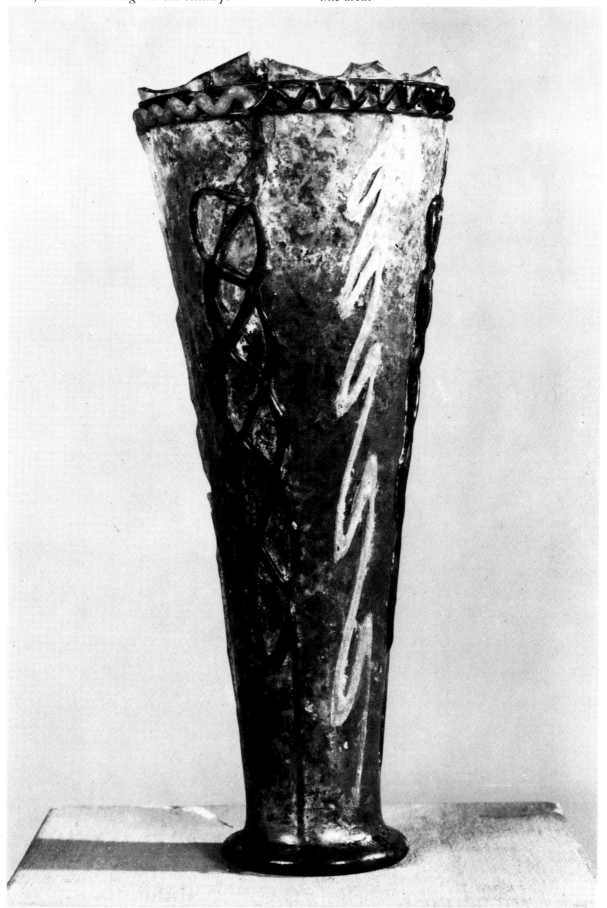

Below *A small jar of pale greenish translucent glass with some surface iridescence, also from the Seine/Rhine area. The outside is decorated with two rows of prunts which are drawn upwards.*

Opposite *A blown vessel from the Seine/Rhine area made in the 5th to the 7th centuries* AD. *This type is known as a bell beaker. The thick walls of brownish-green glass contain many air bubbles.*

Below *An impressive 15th-century Venetian goblet with a green bucket bowl decorated in coloured enamels on a high-drawn ribbed pedestal foot.*

Opposite *A Venetian covered goblet of the 16th century. The cover, bowl and foot is in vetro-di-trina (lace glass). The serpentine motif of the stem is repeated on the cover.*

Venice

VENICE was the seat of the greatest glass-making tradition of all, and no matter how scanty one's knowledge of the city it must inevitably be associated with canals and glass-making. Indeed, few visitors leave without making the trip to Murano and its glassworks. The quality of its modern output may be influenced by the demands of the tourist trade, but nevertheless the glassworkers of Murano are the inheritors of the finest tradition of glassmaking since the material was first dis-covered.

The pre-eminence of Venice came about through a chain of circumstances. The acci-dents of geography, time, political power and the rebirth of the arts produced in Venice a standard of glassmaking both of quality and imagination which the world had not seen before, and has seldom seen since.

Let us look in some detail at how this chain of circumstances occurred. On the face of it, a lagoon of low-lying swampy islands was an unlikely place to create a city. The problems of construction, communication and health would make any site on firm ground seem more favourable, but the earliest settlers were probably refugees from the effects of the barbarian invasions which swept the area after the fall of the Roman Empire. In such a place they would be tolerably safe from attack, and if the site was of no use or interest to anyone else, so much the better. Being thus safe to establish itself, the city of Venice slowly took root in the mud.

As we have noticed in various other areas, turbulent and troubled times had an inhibiting effect on the practice of the domestic arts and crafts. If Venice was able to establish herself while the surrounding region was in a state of turmoil she would become a magnet for the makers of such fragile objects as glass vessels. She would offer a refuge where they could practise their art with the minimum of inter-ference. Glassmaking had, in any event, been known in the region since very early times.

The earliest Venetian wares were undistin-guished and are impossible to differentiate from any other glass of the period. That the glassmakers did flourish was certain, because by 1271 the first records of a glassmakers' guild appear, and shortly afterwards they moved to the island of Murano. This could have been for a variety of reasons. It has been suggested that the glassworks scattered throughout Venice had become a dangerous fire hazard

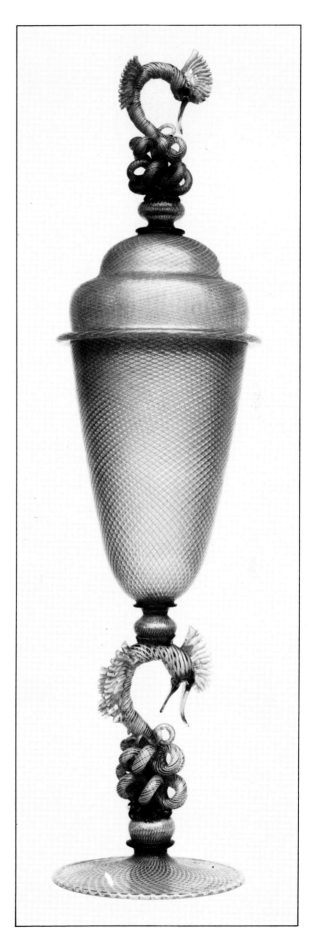

on small and densely populated islands, and their removal to a separate island would benefit all. It may be that having become important and powerful enough to form a guild it was felt that a better control could be maintained over the industry if all the artisans were assembled in one locality.

That the glassmakers were highly regarded is certain. The city records show that some of the glassmakers became powerful and important men, ranking with the nobility in a city that had a highly developed class system.

As communication and trade improved and developed throughout Europe, Venice and Genoa became natural focal points for the trade routes of the world. There was intense rivalry between the two cities, but Venice eventually emerged the victor. She then became the crossroads for land and sea traffic from East to West and North to South. With this position secured her coffers swelled with the taxes and duties she levied on commercial traffic, and Venice became the most powerful city-state in the Mediterranean. Venetian merchants travelled the trade routes of the world and were the main suppliers to the crusades. In the course of their visits to the Middle East they would have had dealings with the Syrian and Mesopotamian glassmakers and the best of Middle Eastern glass would find its way back to Venice to grace the tables of its wealthy inhabitants.

With the overthrow of Islam at the beginning of the 15th century, the decline of the glass trade in the Middle East left a vacuum in the supply of quality glass. Since Venice was in control of all the main commercial routes and had also built up a considerable glass trade of her own, it was natural that she should step in to fill the breach.

In the face of the onslaught of the barbarian hordes the local inhabitants would flee wherever they could find refuge, and what more natural than that glassmakers would make for a place where, from contact with visiting merchants, they knew there would be opportunities to continue the practice of their skills. So as well as having new markets opened to it, Venice also had an infusion of the skills of the Middle East.

The last link in the chain of events that brought Venice to her peak was now about to be forged. This was the rebirth of artistic endeavour and achievement, the Renaissance. The world was once again becoming a more settled place, and prosperity was increasing. For the last few centuries great artistic achieve-

ments had been few and far between, but now there were men ready and willing to patronize the arts, and men of a variety of talents able to satisfy the aesthetic demands of a new society.

Venice was jealous of her position in the world's markets, and to ensure that she kept it highly restrictive conditions were placed on her craftsmen, especially on the glassmakers. They were forbidden under pain of death to practise their skills anywhere outside Venice, or to impart their skills to anyone other than Venetians. The demand for Venetian glassware, however, throughout the courts of Europe, was such that considerable inducements were offered to persuade Venetian glassworkers to risk the consequences and set up their glass pots outside Venice. There are records of Venetian ambassadors using bribery and blackmail to persuade the unfortunate truants to return home. The tide could not be entirely stemmed, and slowly but surely at other glass centres throughout Europe the the Venetian style, generally known as *façon*

Left *A fine example of early Venetian craftsmanship. This ewer shows the effectiveness of coloured enamels applied to coloured glass. Dating from the 15th century, it demonstrates the influence of the Syrian taste both in shape and in decoration.*

Opposite *A Venetian 15th-century goblet of very elegant proportions. The clear glass has a bluish tinge, and the bowl, pedestal and cover are all ribbed. The tall, narrow pedestal gives an indication of the impending change to separate stem and foot.*

Below *A tazza, or shallow cup on a pedestal base, made in Venice in the 16th century. The rim and the edge of the foot are turned to give extra strength, and the purple-blue glass is decorated with gilding and a band of grapes and vine leaves in green and white enamel.*

de Venise, was introduced, but with each country showing just that individuality of style which marked its production from the genuine Venetian.

Inevitably Venice made enemies who considered her power too great, or whose interests conflicted with her own. As a result there were many attempts made to break her influence, and the beginning of the end was in sight when the Portuguese found a new route to the Far East via the Cape of Good Hope at the end of the 16th century. Goods could be shipped direct to and from the East without the necessity of paying high duties to ship them through Venice. Her importance on the trade routes undermined, Venice started to decline, and the Republic finally collapsed in 1797. Long before this the glass trade in Northern Europe had overtaken the Venetian manufacture, and from the end of the 17th century she had lost her important position. However, during the years of her ascendancy, the mid-15th to mid-17th centuries, the glassware of Venice achieved an originality of design and a quality of manufacture which were without equal anywhere in the civilized world. In addition, although she was subsequently overtaken in glassmaking, the effect she had on the production of fine glassware in other countries was distinctive and lasting.

Having looked at some of the causes behind the rise and fall of Venetian glassmaking, what of the glass itself?

As mentioned already, fine glassware does not make its appearance in Venice until the mid-15th century, some time after the fall of Islam. The earliest pieces of any quality were goblets, usually flat-bottomed and with straight tapering sides mounted on a pedestal foot. They are made of coloured glass, usually blue or green, with enamelled decoration round the bowl.

Prior to this time stemmed glasses had been few and far between, but now the Venetian glassmakers started to produce drinking vessels on stems. At first the bowl was set on a plain ribbed pedestal in which stem and foot were one. These pedestals became taller and were decorated with hollow blown bulbs called knops, until for the first time glasses with separate stems and feet appeared. Once it was accepted that the stem and foot could be made in separate pieces there was no limit to the ingenuity that could be used in fashioning the stem: hollow knops with moulded lion masks, stems with a central feature of glass threads drawn out in the shape of serpents or

A flask in opaque coloured glass made to imitate agate. This technique was invented in the East before the Christian era and revived in Venice about 1500, where it was called calcedonio.

A Venetian goblet with an elaborate stem which includes all the features to be found on glasses of the period: blown and moulded hollow knops, loops with pincered trailing and drawn spikes. This is a true showpiece of 17th-century glass.

figures-of-eight, winged stems with pincered fringes, and many others.

In a further development the Venetians improved their clear glass by the addition of lime to the soda-silicate mixture, and produced a fine clear glass which they called *cristallo*. However, it depended in part for its clarity on the thinness with which it was blown. One of the great abilities of the Venetian glassmakers was their skill in the manipulation of the material. They acquired a dexterity in controlling the molten metal which enabled them to produce glasses of a delicacy and with a degree of elaborate decoration that no one else could imitate. Glassware like this was made for a wealthy and sophisticated market, and outside Venice that would mean principally the nobility of Europe. Thus Venetian glass was for a long time the prerogative of the rich and educated.

After the goblets came plates, *tazzas*, flasks, chalices and a wide variety of other domestic vessels in glass. These were made in coloured or clear glass and were decorated with enamelling, gilding and occasionally engraving, although the very thin glass did not really lend itself to the latter medium. A scale pattern was a favourite form of enamelling.

The Venetian craftsmen re-introduced glass made of coloured pastes fused together to imitate marble or chalcedony, which the Romans had made 1500 years earlier. Elaborate decanters called *aquamaniles* or *nefs,* with a canopy of threads of glass, were popular.

One of their greatest achievements was the invention of clear glass incorporating a pattern of opaque white or coloured threads which is called *latticino* or *vetro-di-trina* (lace glass). It was made by affixing a series of glass rods containing the twisted white threads to the outside of the gathering from which the vessel was to be blown. These rods assumed the same temperature as the gather, and when it was blown and marvered would blend into the body of the vessel to produce the pattern. This method was developed to the point where the whole vessel could be entirely covered with a close pattern of these threads.

There were, of course, other glassmaking centres in Italy during this period. The principal ones were at Altare, near Genoa, Florence, and Naples. But Venice with its domination of world trade routes and the highly developed skills of its craftsmen became the centre of glass production which made the most dramatic and lasting impression on the history of glass through the ages.

This covered 16th-century Venetian bowl illustrates clearly several methods of decoration. It has moulded ribs on the pedestal and cover; applied prunts in blue and purple glass; applied enamel decoration in green and white, and gilding on the ribs.

A Spanish 18th-century oil lamp with four spouts. This piece has an excess of applied decoration which fails to hide the crudeness of its manufacture.

A Spanish ewer of the 16th century, from the Barcelona area. The green and white enamel decoration shows a fusion of Moorish and Christian styles.

Spain

THE art of glassmaking was very active in Spain over many centuries, but for the most part Spaniards were imitators rather than innovators. Their glass acquired a certain native character, but could never compete with the more desirable product of the other glass-producing centres already discussed. For this reason Spanish glass tends to be much less known and appreciated by collectors today.

Glassmaking was introduced to Spain by the Romans, and it is unlikely that the glass being made in the country at that time would differ very much from that being made in Italy. In 711, after the collapse of the Roman Empire, the country was invaded by the Moors from North Africa. The strife continued for about 200 years until the 10th century, when Spain became settled under a strong Muslim influence. The Syrian and subsequently the Islamic styles which they introduced were noticeable in the glassware that was made throughout the occupation, and indeed lasted into the 18th century, long after the Moors had finally been defeated.

In the 16th century the Venetian influence made itself felt, and was superimposed on the Muslim style to produce a native style. This infusion from Venice arrived from two sources, directly from Italy by way of the Venetian and Altarist glassworkers, and also from the Low Countries. In the year 1516 Charles V became king of both Spain and the Netherlands. He encouraged the development of *façon de Venise* in Spain, and introduced glassmakers from the Low Countries, who were also at that time turning out glass in the Venetian style.

From the 15th century onwards there is evidence of a thriving glass industry in Spain. Fairs were held in Barcelona for the glass-houses to exhibit their wares, and descriptions exist of whole streets lined with stalls displaying glass of all types. This flourishing trade may have been partly due to the fact that raw materials were plentiful and of good quality. Spain provided one of the principal sources of soda ash for the Venetian glass trade; this was barilla, which was obtained by burning a species of salt marsh plant.

There were three principal glass-producing areas in Spain–Catalonia, the area around Barcelona; Andalusia, the region around Granada and Castile; and the area about Madrid.

Andalusian glass production was most strongly affected by the Moorish influence, and the wares of this region differ noticeably from those made further north. The glass generally was made of bubbly green tinted metal and was distinguished by its applied ornament. This took the form of a profusion of applied loop handles, pincered trails and spikes. Jugs, vases, bowls, beakers and lamps were among the wide range of vessels produced. Other types of decoration were seldom used, but occasionally pieces have been found with a thick overlay of dark coloured glass, usually brown, black or purple.

The glassmakers of Catalonia managed to free themselves of the Moorish influence much earlier than the Andalusians, and during the 16th and 17th centuries built up a reputation for good quality glassware in the Venetian style. A glassmakers' guild existed in Barcelona from 1594 which not only controlled the manufacturers in the same way that the Venetian trade was managed, but also licensed the retailers.

One remnant of the Syrian taste in design which was grafted on to the Venetian style was the use of enamelled decoration. The method used was to cover almost the whole surface of the vessel with patterns of leaves, branches, flowers and birds in thickly applied enamels of green, white and yellow. This combination of manufacturing and decorative styles is very distinctive and easily recognizable. After 1650 the importance of Catalonian glass seems to have declined, and although much glass continued to be made, quality was sacrificed for quantity.

The output of the Castilian glasshouses was also considerable, but it was not until the 18th century that it achieved any real distinction. Until that time Castilian glassmakers seemed content to follow the lead of other centres, both domestic and foreign. By the early 18th century the clear engraved glass of Bohemia had become popular in Spain, and in 1720 Juan Goyeneche set up a glasshouse at Nuevo Baztan to produce it locally. He became the first man to introduce engraving into Spain. There is also a record of an Englishman offering to introduce the manufacture of crystal glass at about the same period, which may well have been the lead glass of Ravenscroft. It would appear, however, that the quality that Goyeneche sought eluded him, and his glasshouse lasted only about eight years.

In 1728 Ventura Sit, who had worked for Goyeneche, set up a glassworks of his own

which obtained royal patronage and became the royal glass factory at La Granja de Don Idelfonso. It was considered by many members of the European nobility to be a status symbol to support a factory turning out high quality but uneconomic domestic wares. This famous factory was supported by Philip V, who financed it until about 1760 when the expense became too great. The speciality of La Granja was mirrors, all of which Philip reserved for his own use, but the cost of making them was so enormous that he could eventually no longer bear the expense.

In addition to the mirrors a wide variety of tableware was produced, which was enriched with engraving, gilding and enamelling. In about 1760 the production of the factory was offered for public sale, but the prices were too high, and in 1762 the factory was given the exclusive right to sell glass in Madrid. Because of the distance of Madrid from the sea and the hazards of road transport in those days, export was an unprofitable business.

In 1809 Joseph Bonaparte, who was installed as king of Spain by Napoleon, ordered the sale of the factory, and during the next few years it seems to have passed through a variety of ownerships, but it never regained the reputation it had achieved under royal patronage in the 18th century.

Opposite *An 18th-century Spanish jug in white opal glass with painted decoration.*

Below *A good example of an engraved decanter made at the royal factory of La Granja de Don Idelfonso, Spain, in the 18th century.*

China

BEFORE continuing with the story of the development of glass in the Western world, this is a convenient point in our narrative to consider the manufacture of glass in the Far East.

The cultural history of China goes back about 4000 years, and during that time she has been the originator of many of the domestic arts, and has embellished them with a skill which has seldom been equalled. The casting and decorating of bronzes, the invention of porcelain, the delicate carving of ivory, wood and precious stones, painting and enamelling are some of the fields in which China has excelled. In view of all this it seems strange that the art of glassmaking was never developed to the same high degree. Glassmaking is essentially a skill born of and developed by the Western world, and China, probably due to her infrequent contact with the West until comparatively recent times, has never acquired the feel for it.

Left *A Chinese bottle made in the 18th century with blue over a white ground. The blue layer is cut away in a pattern of lotus flowers to expose the white beneath. This is the cameo technique which was used to produce the Portland vase (see page 11).*

Above *An 18th-century glass vessel in the shape of a Ku (a type of ritual vessel traditional in China). Early Kus were in bronze, and the green colour of this one has an affinity with the green patina which these bronze vessels acquired.*

Opposite top *An 18th-century Chinese vase with a red layer over a yellow ground. The red layer is cut into a pattern of peonies.*

Opposite below *A small moulded bowl made in China in the 19th century. The marbled green and aubergine colour, which is reminiscent of natural stone, illustrates the Chinese attitude to glass— it was regarded as a substitute for natural materials, rather than an end in itself.*

Written records suggest that the knowledge of glass manufacture arrived from the West in the 15th century AD, but glass was imported into China long before the start of the Christian era, and tombs of the Chou and Han dynasties have yielded beads and small moulded tomb figures of undoubted Chinese manufacture which are copies of imported wares. These were probably made in glass as a substitute for jade or crystal.

A very few pieces of glass have been found which can be ascribed to the period up to the 17th century, when a glassworks was set up in Peking under the royal patronage of the Emperor K'ang Hsi. At that time there were Jesuit priests living in Peking, and one of their leaders was Dutch. Since glassmaking was an important and highly developed industry in Holland at that time, it is possible that this workshop may have been set up with assistance and instructions from the Jesuits. A number of examples from this period exist today and coloured glass, cameo glass and clear glass were all made, although some of them show the effects of "crizzling".

Glass manufacture has continued in China up to the present day, and most of that which turns up is 19th or early 20th century. The shapes produced are usually copies of porcelain or bronze vessels, and usually in monochrome. A wide variety of colours was used, including blue, yellow, green, amethyst, brown, white and black. Apart from the distinctive shapes, the walls of Chinese glass vessels are usually much thicker than would be found in Euro-pean glass, and the colours are generally opaque and have an oily appearance.

Carving on Chinese glass is generally executed in the same style as that found on jade or rock crystal, and it is clear that glass was regarded as a substitute for those materials rather than an artistic medium in its own right. Flower sprays, fish and dragons are typical decorative subjects to be found on Chinese glass.

Of particular interest are snuff bottles which were made in three- or four-colour overlay and then carved, or of clear glass decorated with delicate painting on the inside surfaces. The variety of these is remarkable and the work-manship often exquisite.

The manipulative possibilities of glass never seem to have captured the Chinese imagination, and it is clear that they have always only regarded it as a substitute for natural stone.

Above *Chinese bowl, 17th–18th centuries, in glass which was originally clear but which now suffers from crizzling. The decoration is cut.*

Right *Dark blue mould-blown Chinese vase, 17th–18th centuries, with four panels, each containing a peach.*

Britain – the early years

THE early development of glass in the British Isles is open to much speculation. Specimens exist of some periods, but there is no sure evidence of where they were made. At other times there is ample documentary proof that glass was being made, but so far no examples have been found that can be related to that evidence.

The earliest glass to be seen in Britain was probably brought there by the Romans, although one may speculate whether the Phoenicians, prior to the Romans, could have brought vessels of glass when they came to barter with the natives for tin.

There is no evidence of glass being made in England either during the Roman occupation or for several centuries after the fall of the Roman Empire, but from the number of glass vessels which have been recovered from graves it is possible that some was made in the south of England. The problem is that styles were so consistent over a large area that it is not normally possible to identify the production of a particular locality.

Claw beakers, cone beakers and palm cups are typical of the Seine-Rhine period, and from the quantity found in England they may well have been produced there. During the 8th to the 10th centuries there is evidence that continental glassworkers, probably French, were brought to England to make window glass for churches, and after the Norman invasion when the great vogue for church building got under way this trade would have increased.

The first glassmaker working in England whose name is recorded was Laurence Vitrearius of Normandy who obtained a grant of land at Dyers Cross in Sussex in 1220. In 1240 he was commissioned by Henry III to make both plain and coloured glass for Westminster Abbey. Succeeding generations of the family were recorded until 1301. Then in about 1343 one John Schurterre settled at Chiddingfold in Sussex and became the most important glassmaker in England. This part of Sussex remained for a long time the centre of English glassmaking, and in this context it is interesting to note that a Venetian map of England published in the 16th century shows only two places as making glass, one at Guildford and the other at Chiddingfold, where the remains of a number of old glasshouses have been excavated.

Apart from the window glass, simple glass vessels were also made which were hawked around the countryside. A succession of French glassworkers arrived to carry on the trade, but there are no records of native-born Englishmen being engaged in its manufacture. The tradition during this period was that of the potash-based glass of the *Waldglas* type commonly being produced in France and Germany at the same time. The rate at which wood was consumed to support this type of manufacture was eventually to bring about the downfall of the French glassworkers in Sussex.

During the first half of the 16th century there was a further influx of French glassworkers, this time from Lorraine, but it appears that they were not popular, and eventually they spread out and settled in other parts of the country. The main cause of the trouble was the rate at which the forests were being destroyed. The glassmakers were in competition with the ironworkers for wood as fuel; the latter, however, were static while the glassworkers with their much lighter glass pots could move on whenever the local supplies of fuel were exhausted. Finally the ironworkers petitioned for the ban on the use of wood by the glassmakers. By the early 17th century coal was coming into use as an alternative fuel, and in 1615 the use of wood was ended. This encouraged the dispersal of the French and led them to settle in districts where coal was readily available such as Stourbridge and Newcastle, where their influence was to be felt for 200 years or more.

One of the Lorraine glassmakers was Jean Carré who, in 1567, obtained a licence for twenty-one years to set up a glasshouse in London, where he undertook to produce glass as good as the Venetian glass which was then so highly regarded. To this end he imported several Venetian glassmakers, and is the first manufacturer in England recorded as having used soda (which the Venetians used) instead of potash.

When Carré died in 1572 one of his Venetian craftsmen, Jacob Verzelini, took over the licence and in 1575 acquired a monopoly to manufacture glass. Only a handful of glasses exist today which can be attributed to the Verzelini glasshouse. They are all goblets in the *façon de Venise*, engraved in diamond point and bearing dates between 1577 and 1586. Verzelini ran the glasshouse for seventeen years before retiring, and he finally died a rich and respected citizen of London in 1606.

With Verzelini's retirement the monopoly to make glass in England passed through several hands until Sir Robert Mansell gained control in 1618. He was successful as a result of the law of 1615 banning the use of wood for firing glass pots, since he had acquired the patents covering the use of coal as a fuel for this purpose. He maintained control over the industry for about thirty years.

During the Civil War and the Commonwealth (1640–60) glassmaking suffered, and it was only on the restoration of Charles II in 1660 that it once again started to flourish, this time under the influence of the Duke of Buckingham, although he never secured the totally monopolistic power of his predecessors. In 1664 the Glass Sellers Company was formed, and from then on the trade was largely dictated by the company. Two things illustrate this clearly. There still exists today part of the correspondence between John Greene, a glass seller in London, and Allesio Morelli in Venice. Greene bought glass from Morelli, and in his letters he states exactly how his orders are to be executed, often complaining of the quality he had received, and enclosing sketches of the shapes and styles he requires to be supplied. The other instance concerns the backing of

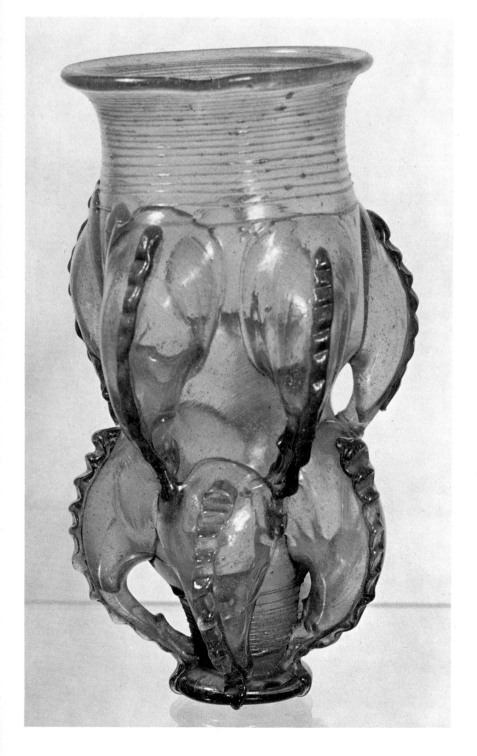

George Ravenscroft by the Glass Sellers Company to pursue his research into the development of a new kind of glass. They agreed to finance him on condition that when it was proved successful he would manufacture glass to the specifications which they would provide.

Thus the glass trade had changed in 100 years from an industry based on individual semi-itinerant glassmakers to a properly organized and commercial enterprise controlled by a regular trade association. This was to prove the springboard for the ascendency of English glass over the next 150 years.

English–Ravenscroft to 1850

VENETIAN glass was thinly blown and delicate, and fine pieces executed for wealthy families were undoubtedly treasured and carefully preserved, so that many of them have lasted until the present time, but glass made for everyday use did not receive the same attention, and little of it has survived. Indirectly George Ravenscroft was to change this, and thus relatively large quantities of 18th-century domestic glass exist today.

Ravenscroft was born in 1618 into a family

Opposite far left *A claw beaker with trailed thread applied to the neck, and two rows of hollow prunts.*

Opposite middle *A goblet and cover made of lead glass in England about 1680. The Venetian influence is still very noticeable in this piece.*

Above *A jar of squat form made from blue glass containing many small air bubbles. The outside is decorated with trailing. It was found in Essex, England and dates from the 7th century.*

that must have been reasonably affluent, since records refer to the male members as "Gent." or "Esq.". He was not a glassmaker, and reached the age of fifty-five before he set up a glasshouse at the Savoy in London to carry out experiments to find a new form of glass. The late 17th century was a period of intense research and experiment by men of culture and education to advance scientific knowledge for the benefit of their fellow men. The Royal Society was a product of this era. Ravenscroft's experiments showed such promise that in 1674 the Glass Sellers Company set him up in a glasshouse in Henley-on-Thames to pursue his researches in seclusion. He also took the precaution of obtaining a seven-year patent on his new ideas.

By 1676 he had made such progress that the Glass Sellers issued a certificate expressing their satisfaction with his "glass of flint" as he called it, and gave him permission to identify his glass by means of a seal bearing a raven's head. It is by this device that a small number of glass vessels can be attributed to Ravenscroft's glasshouses. His secret was the addition of lead oxide to the other raw materials, which produced a soft and brilliant metal of great reflective quality. The Venetian *cristallo* had looked clear and white partly on account of its thinness, but this new material remained clear and transparent when much thicker sections were blown. In its early years Ravenscroft's new glass suffered from a defect known as crizzling, which produced a cloudy effect in the metal, and was due to an imbalance in the mixture, but this problem was finally solved.

Ravenscroft terminated his agreement with the Glass Sellers Company in 1679 and died in 1681 about the same time that his patent expired. His glasshouse was continued by Hawley Bishopp, who had worked with him at Henley on behalf of the Glass Sellers, and who presumably had the formula for his new glass, but before many years had passed, lead glass was in common use in all the glassmaking centres of England.

For the first few years after its introduction glass vessels continued to be made in the Venetian tradition. Indeed, Ravenscroft had imported two Venetian glassmakers to work in his Savoy works. As early as 1670 the designs which Greene had sent to Venice had shown a tendency to simplify the Venetian styles, and as time went by several factors helped to create a particularly English style. As the demand for glass grew, and new glasshouses opened, there could never have been enough skilled Venetian workers to staff them.

A Roemer *with ribbed bowl, stem and foot, made in the glasshouse of George Ravenscroft about 1680. The stem has applied prunts, the* lower one in the centre bearing an impressed mark of a raven's head; his trade mark.

Below *A Newcastle light baluster wine glass with a coat-of-arms by the Beilby family, who specialized in this method in Newcastle during the 1760s and 1770s. The rim is gilded.*

This meant that more and more Englishmen had to be trained, and it is unlikely that they would have acquired and imitated exactly the abilities of their Venetian teachers.

The difference between the new glass of lead and the soda *cristallo* was considerable. In the molten state it has been described as being the difference between cold and hot treacle. The lead glass did not lend itself to the extravagances of the Venetian style, and because of its lustre plainer shapes made as effective a display as the more elaborate Venetian shapes.

The Glass Sellers Company, being a commercial organization, would undoubtedly have looked for wider markets, and this could be achieved by making the glass both cheaper and more durable. The quicker a glass vessel could be produced the cheaper it would be, and the less ornate it was the more practicable it would be in use.

During the period under review the various changes of style and decoration follow each other in a regular sequence which has been very well catalogued by E. Barrington-Haynes (*Glass Through the Ages*). The transitional period from about 1680 to 1690 is usually referred to as Anglo-Venetian, when such Venetian characteristics as spiked gadroons, trailed decoration and pincered stems still appear on glasses. These gradually disappeared to give way to the first period which can be described as being peculiarly English, the period of heavy baluster stems, 1690–1725. The knop formations on the stems of these glasses derive from the hollow blown knopped stems of Venetian glasses, and are the last signs of Venetian influence on English glass. The stems of English glasses are either solid or contain air bubbles, usually called tears. The early baluster stem glasses are notable for their size and weight. Some examples are more than 12 inches high and weigh about 10 pounds. The bowls are usually solid at the base, and the knops appear in a variety of forms with such descriptive names as cylinder knop, egg knop, acorn knop and mushroom knop. As time passed the proportions of these glasses became more refined; height increased, weight decreased, and where the stem had previously been made with one knop, combinations of knops became fashionable. This style reached its peak with wine glasses made in the Newcastle glasshouses. The Newcastle light baluster is a style much sought after by collectors: tall, with multi-knopped stems often containing rows of tiny air beads, and of clear white metal.

Opposite bottom *English blue glass. Left to right: a decanter of about 1780; a custard glass of about 1760 with a ribbed bowl on a plain foot; a wine glass of about 1780 with a facet-cut stem.*

Below *A bottle attributed to the Nailsea glassworks near Bristol. The dark brown glass is flecked with white, and applied to the surface are vertical trails of pincered brown glass.*

One of the best known glassmaking families in Newcastle at this period was that of Dagnia. They were of Italian origin, and appear to have arrived in Newcastle from Bristol in about 1684. Until that time only sheet glass and bottles were made in Newcastle, and it is very probable that the Dagnias brought with them the new lead glass and started the quality glass trade which culminated in the fine wine glasses already referred to.

It is interesting to consider the question of metal for a moment. Most early lead glass shows distinct tinges of colour, usually black, green or yellow, which are the result of impurities in the raw materials. Undoubtedly the glassmakers endeavoured to produce metal that was colourless (white) and added various chemicals to counteract these natural impurities, but it was very much a matter of guesswork, and success was arrived at more by chance than by precise chemical control. One way to make success more likely was to use sand that was known to be largely free from impurities.

This occurred near Kings Lynn in Norfolk, and also near Newcastle. Sand from these areas was in great demand, and was shipped to all the English glassmaking centres.

Contemporary with the baluster period was another group of glasses which owe their introduction to the accession of George I in 1714 to the throne of England. To mark this event glasses with so-called "Silesian" stems were produced. These had tapering, four-sided moulded stems which the English glassmakers soon modified to have six and eight sides. These retained their popularity along with the baluster glasses until the introduction of the first glass Excise Act of 1745. This imposed a duty of nine shillings and fourpence per hundredweight on the raw material used in glassmaking, and had a drastic effect on the glass trade. Glassware became plainer in shape and lighter in weight to minimize the effect of the tax. This resulted in the introduction of plain stemmed glasses which contained less lead than previously.

Here we see a group of English 18th-century wine glasses. Left *A knopped stem with ribbed bowl and foot, made about 1730.* Middle *This piece, made about 1720 to commemorate the accession of* King George I, *has a square knop over an eight-sided stem.* Right *A composite air-twist stem glass with a ball bowl and domed foot, made about 1750.*

From the mid-18th century onwards public taste changed, and the more ornate rococo and *chinoiserie* styles became popular. This had its effect on glassware, and the manufacturers changed their styles to meet the demand. From 1750 onwards air-twist and opaque twist stems make their appearance. Both these styles were suited to an art which put a premium on the amount of raw material used, since they permitted decorative glass to be made without the large quantities of raw material of the baluster stem period.

Air-twist stems were made by trapping a pattern of air bubbles in the metal from which the stem was to be drawn. As this was pulled and twisted the bubbles were transformed into long spiral threads of air. Opaque twist stems were made by implanting a pattern of white or coloured enamel glass rods into a block of clear glass, which was then drawn out and twisted in the same manner as the air twists. Both these styles flourished until 1777 when a further duty was imposed on the enamel rods used to produce the opaque twist stems. As a consequence the twist stems fell from favour, and cutting began to emerge as the main form of decoration.

Cutting of glass, by imported German craftsmen, had been popular early in the 18th century, but because of the weight of glass required to produce cut pieces, the 1745 Excise Duty had ended that. In the 1770s cutting again became popular, but this time as a method of decorating the stems of glasses with facets. The plain stems were cut with a series of scallops so that the intersecting edges formed diamonds or hexagons. The use of cutting spread so that from 1780 onwards a wide range of glassware was being made with more and more elaborate cut decoration. Cutting exploited the lustrous and reflective qualities of lead glass, and for the next fifty years English glassmaking reached the peak of quality in both metal and decoration. An early 19th-century dining table set with a service of cut glass shining in the light of cut-glass chandeliers must have been an impressive sight. After 1830 styles tended to become fussier and the art generally went into a decline.

I have dealt in some detail with drinking glasses, but throughout the period many other domestic articles were made in glass: chandeliers, candlesticks, jugs, bowls, decanters, bottles, sweetmeat dishes and so on.

Cutting as an applied decoration has already been mentioned, but other forms of decoration are to be seen on glass of the period – engraving, gilding and enamelling. All these were practised in England, but they seldom achieved either the degree of quality or popularity that they attained on the Continent. Engraving on glass is rare in the early 18th century, and when it does start to make an appearance after 1730, wheel engraving is the method generally preferred. Diamond point engraving by English artists in the 18th century is virtually unknown. On the other hand, large quantities of the fine Newcastle light balusters were exported and most of those which survive today carry Dutch engraving, both wheel and diamond point, which is of a very high standard indeed.

Gilding occurs either as oil gilding, which is not permanent and is by now usually badly rubbed or barely distinguishable, or gilding which was fired on to produce a permanent decoration. James Giles, a London engraver and decorator, executed a number of glasses in the latter method, and his style, consisting of sprays of flowers and insects, is easily recognizable. In the last quarter of the 18th century the Jacobs family in Bristol also turned out a lot of gilded glassware. Unusually, many of their pieces are signed.

Enamelling was only carried out by a very few artists. The bulk of what remains today is attributed either to Michael Edkins or to the Beilby family, although there are a few enamelled glasses that do not conform to the style of either of these. The glass attributed to Edkins is nearly all opaque white glass which was made in Stourbridge or Bristol. This was a dense white material made to resemble porcelain. Edkins is recorded as having worked in both towns, and the decoration consists of birds, flowers and *chinoiserie* subjects.

The Beilby family, brother and sister, worked in Newcastle from 1762 to 1778. They painted mainly in white enamel, small scenes of rural pursuits or classical ruins on sets of wine glasses. The family must have been widely known and highly regarded, since a small number of goblets exists today which

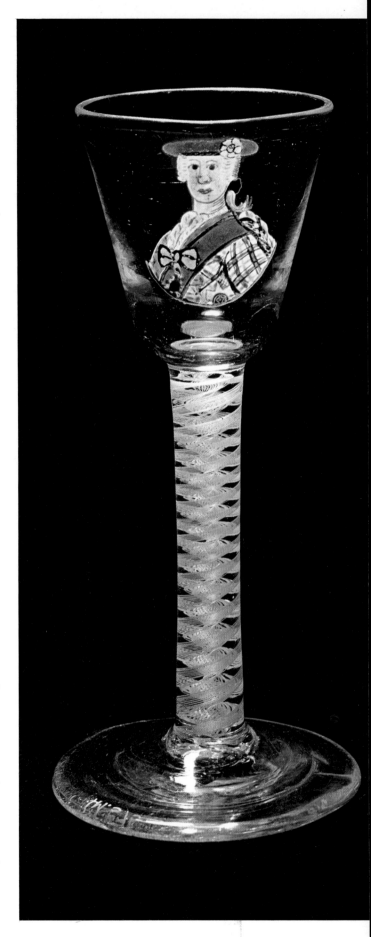

carry coats of arms in polychrome decoration. These were executed to special orders for titled families.

So far only clear glass has been discussed, but there was a demand for coloured glass as well. While early 18th-century pieces do exist they are rare, and the bulk of the coloured glass which has come down to us dates from the late 18th and early 19th centuries. The principal colours are green, blue and amethyst, while amber and red are rare.

One useful means of dating glass is presented by reference to the many pieces which were engraved to commemorate some person or event. The reference may be to a person who is unknown to us, but a date is given which enables us to place the item. Alternatively the engraving may illustrate a person or event which is well known, and thus give an indication of the date of the glass. Probably the best known English glasses are those relating to the Jacobite movement from the failure of the rebellion of 1745 to the death of Prince Charles Edward in 1788. During this period several societies sympathetic to the Jacobite cause flourished, and it was fashionable to drink a toast to Bonnie Prince Charlie from glasses bearing his portrait or other emblems representative of the movement. Occasionally there were also added Latin mottoes expressing hope for his return; among these are FIAT, AUDENTIOR IBO, and REVIRESCAT.

In this chapter we have seen how, during the 18th century, the English glass trade developed its own tradition which, while it owed its inspiration to Venetian, German and French ideas, managed to evolve an idiom which was independent of any of them, to the extent that English glass was highly regarded abroad and exported in huge quantities.

Left *A wine glass with an opaque-twist stem bearing a portrait in coloured enamels of "Bonnie Prince Charlie". There were many glasses made in the mid-18th century which were decorated with Jacobite sentiments. Most of them are symbolic—portrait glasses are rare.*

Top *A cruet bottle in dark blue glass, faceted and gilded. One of the best-known gilders was James Giles, who worked in London in the 1760s. The cruet, of which the stopper is missing, was made about 1770.*

Right *Another example of a Jacobite portrait glass, diamond-engraved.*

A wine glass with a knopped stem engraved with a portrait of the famous actress Sarah Siddons (1755–1831).

A cordial glass of about 1760, with a straight-sided bowl and a white air-twist stem, enamelled with garlands.

Below *A fine English baluster-stem goblet, made about 1700. The engraving, in diamond point, shows Adam and Eve in the Garden of* Eden. *This is a rare piece, as diamond-point engraving is uncommon at this period.*

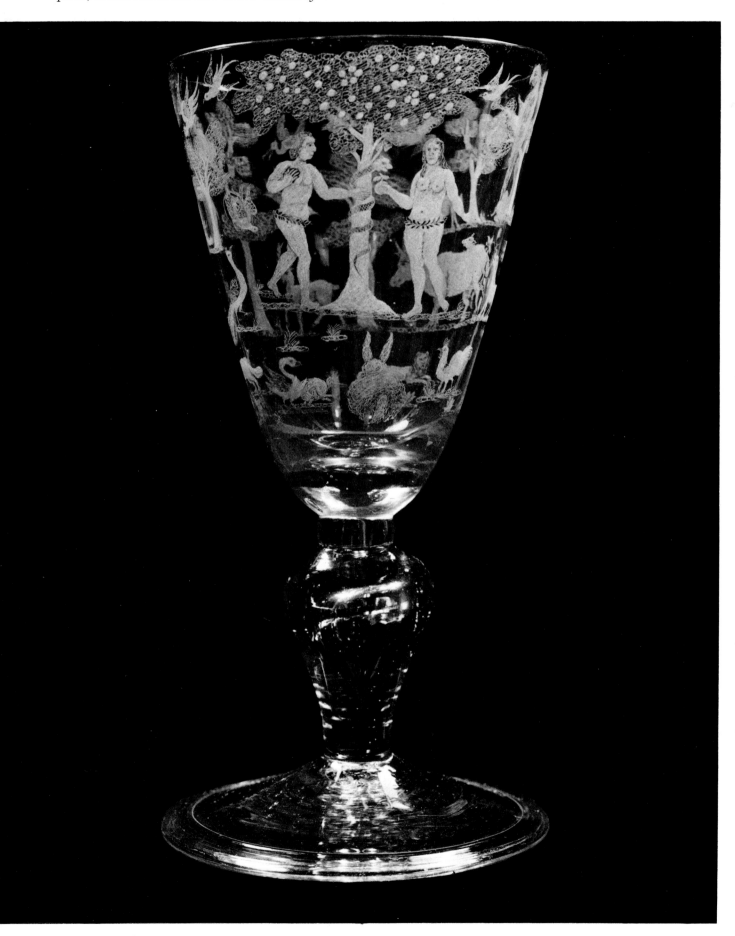

Below *A cruet set of about 1760 in opaque white glass made in Stourbridge and Bristol to imitate porcelain. The name of Michael Edkins is associated with this style of decoration.*

Opposite *A canoe-shaped bowl of about 1800 on a pedestal. The bowl is elaborately cut, and the shape is particularly associated with the Irish glasshouses.*

Ireland

THERE are written references to glassmaking in Ireland from 1258 onwards, when French glassworkers are recorded as operating there. They probably made their way to Ireland from the glassmaking centres in Sussex. In 1586 a Captain Thomas Woodhouse acquired a patent giving him the sole right to make glass in Ireland for eight years, but he does not appear to have been very successful, for in 1589 a George Longe bought out his patent for £300. Longe was an Englishman and a trained glassmaker. He apparently had considerable interests in the glass trade in England, and thus extended his business into Ireland. Longe is also interesting because he is the first recorded Englishman with any great experience as a glassmaker; until this time they are all French or Italian.

The Act of 1615 banning wood for firing glass furnaces in England was not extended to Ireland until 1641, so that it is quite possible that there was a further influx of the French glassworkers from the south of England. After 1641 glassmaking seems to have declined.

The first glasshouse producing lead glass was set up in Dublin in 1690 by a Captain Roche, barely ten years after Ravenscroft's patent had expired. He went into partnership with Richard Fitzsimmons, and this company continued in business until about 1760. At the same time that the Excise Act of 1745 imposed a duty on glass made in England, Irish glass was exempted, but its export was forbidden. This had an inhibiting effect on the Irish trade, since the number of inhabitants of the island able to afford good quality glassware was too small to support any great manufacturing capacity. At the same time the effect on the

home trade was aggravated by the fact that imports from England were not banned. However, in 1780 there occurred the event which was to put new life into the Irish glass trade, the granting of Free Trade and the lifting of all restrictions on the industry.

As explained in an earlier chapter, the use of cutting was becoming fashionable in England at this time, but was inhibited by heavy duties. The English manufacturers therefore saw the creation of Free Trade in Ireland as a golden opportunity to cater for the public demand without having to pay the heavy duties they would incur at home.

The reputation of Irish glass was made from 1780 to about 1830 and glasshouses were started in Cork, Waterford, Dublin and Belfast. Those amongst them which were financed by Irishmen, such as the Penrose brothers at Waterford, relied entirely, in the first instance at least, on imported English craftsmen to produce the glass. In 1825 Irish Free Trade was ended, and the advantage of manufacturing in Ireland was lost. This, combined with an increasing floridity of style, caused a decline in the trade and the importance of Irish glass was finished.

Before the age of cutting the product of the Irish glasshouses was indistinguishable from that of the English factories. After 1780 when cutting became fashionable the same patterns were produced in both countries, but there are some pointers which help to identify the Irish product. Most important among these was the occasional practice of impressing the factory name on the bottom of some tableware, particularly decanters. Thus we sometimes find the names B. Edwards, Belfast; Cork Glass Co., and Penrose Waterford. Certain styles of engraving are associated with particular factories, and some styles of cutting are considered peculiarly Irish.

It has been my experience that, to many people, Irish glass is synonymous with the name Waterford. There is no doubt that the Waterford factory did acquire a very high reputation, but there were others, and for the sake of the record the important ones which were operating between 1780–1850 are listed below:

Waterford Glass House.
Cork Glass Co.
Waterloo Glass House, Cork.
Terrace Glass Works, Cork.

B Edwards, Belfast.
Belfast Glass Works.
Richard Williams & Co., Dublin.
Charles Mulvaney, Dublin.

The history of the Waterford Glass House is well documented with advertisements, factory records and correspondence between members of the Penrose and Gatchell families. It was founded by the brothers George and William Penrose in 1783. They were wealthy men who knew nothing of glassmaking, but could see the opportunities which Free Trade offered. Initially their works was staffed by English craftsmen under the leadership of John Hill of Stourbridge, who was an experienced glassmaker. He stayed for three years and appears to have left under a cloud. Before leaving he handed on his secrets for mixing the raw materials to a clerk with whom he was friendly named Johnathan Gatchell. As the owner of such important information, Gatchell grew to be an important figure in the business, and in 1799 with two partners he bought out the remaining Penrose brother. Thereafter the company remained in the hands of the Gatchell family until it closed in 1851.

Germany

THE next three sections will cover the later development of glass in the area which we looked at in an earlier chapter under the all-embracing title of Seine-Rhine. As different regional styles arose we shall now split it into Germany, Bohemia and the Low Countries. This is a largely arbitrary division for two reasons, the first political and the second artistic.

The national boundaries of Europe are today very different from those which existed prior to the First World War. Few people, I suspect, could accurately place on a modern map of Europe the old principalities of Hesse or Thuringia, to name only two of the independent states which were welded into a unified Germany during the 19th century. For this reason the modern names will do well enough to indicate the areas under discussion. Artistically several of the glass styles (for example the *Roemer*) were common to the whole of northern Europe, but by the 18th century a sufficient number of regional characteristics had developed to justify an examination of each of the areas referred to above on its own merits.

Little is known of glassmaking in Germany from the 8th to the 15th centuries. A few specimens have been found that provide enough information to show that glass was made during this period, but it appears to have been confined to small crudely made vessels of strictly utilitarian purpose. Two items which have come to light are two reliquaries which are important because they contain parchments dated 1282 and 1519. The former was discovered in a church at Michelfeld, near Hall, and is a small jar decorated with trailed threads which immediately takes one's mind back to the trailed-thread snake vases made in Cologne in the 3rd century. The other is a short parallel-sided beaker called an *Igel*. This name means hedgehog, and is derived from the applied decoration, which is a series of spikes reminiscent of the spines of a hedgehog.

These applied knobs of glass are called prunts, or *Nuppen* in German, and are one of the most characteristic features of northern European glass from the late 14th century onwards. It is possible to draw a parallel between these prunts and the projections of the earlier Seine/Rhine claw beakers. Whereas in the early glasses the prunts were hollow blown and drawn out to form the distinctive long claws, the later prunts were restricted to

Opposite bottom *An elaborately decorated German covered goblet of the 18th century. The inverted baluster stem contains air beads, and the engraving on lid, bowl and foot is gilded.*

Below *A large goblet of clear glass with blue overlay made in Germany in the 19th century. The blue layer has been cut away to leave a scene from mythology.*

An enamelled Passglas *divided into six zones. The decoration is in the form of a triumphal procession and the glass, celebrating a baptism, is dated 1662.*

solid lumps of glass which owed their appearance and decorative effects to the manner in which the surface was finished. They were drawn out to produce thin spikes resembling thorns; drawn out and folded over to form loops from which were suspended small rings of glass; drawn into curls and pressed back onto the surface of the vessel to look like pigs' tails. They were also flattened and moulded to produce a beaded surface, when they are commonly called raspberry or strawberry prunts. These last are the ones which are most frequently seen today.

As time passed the squat *Igel* was made taller while retaining its parallel sides, until glasses appeared which were more than 12 inches high. These became very popular and acquired different names according to their intended use or style of decoration. One version decorated with rows of prunts which resembled broken-off leaf stalks was called *Krautstrunk* (cabbage stalk). Another version was a plain glass divided into zones by horizontal trailed rings. This was the *Passglas* which each drinker in turn was expected to drain to the next division in one breath.

During the 16th and 17th centuries these glasses became taller and wider and were called *Humpen*. They were often decorated in coloured enamels and had particular names according to the subject of the decoration. *Reichsadlerhumpen* were painted with the double-headed imperial eagle, and on the outspread wings were painted the coats of arms of the fifty-six members of the Germanic Confederation. The *Kurfürstenhumpen* showed the Emperor and the seven Electors. These were large thinly blown glasses which are rare today. The *Daumenglas* was a more robust barrel-shaped vessel with a series of pockets set into its sides to provide finger grips for the user. They are rather unattractive but technically interesting examples of glassmaking.

Probably the most famous type of glass to appear in northern Europe, and one which is made down to the present day, is the *Roemer*. This originated as a large cup-shaped bowl with a hollow stem which was blown in one piece and mounted on a long narrow pedestal foot made from a thread of glass wound around a conical pattern. The stem section was ornamented with prunts and milled collars at top or bottom. As time went by the foot assumed more importance and grew taller, while the bowl tended to get smaller. In later years the pedestal was formed in one piece with a corrugated outer surface to represent the

54

original thread of glass. Incidentally, the name "rummer" applied to the large beer glasses which first made their appearance in England in the 1780s is said to be a corruption of the name *Roemer*.

Enamelling as a means of decorating glass was very popular in Germany from the early 16th century onwards. The Venetians had supplied enamelled glass for the German market painted with coats of arms, but this is usually easy to distinguish from the domestic product because the German style was more robust with bright colours more heavily laid on. Whatever it lacked in finesse. German enamelling succeeded by its sheer exuberance. *Schwarzlot* was another style of painting on glass which gained some popularity during the 17th century. This consisted of outline pictures in black with the clear areas sometimes filled in with a brown wash. In the latter case the black was applied to one side of the glass while the brown was painted on the other. Johann Schaper (1621–70) produced some very fine examples in this technique.

The Venetian influence was never felt to the same extent in Germany as it was in the Low Countries, but Venetian craftsmen were employed there. One result of this influence, but one which was modified to suit local taste, was the number of elaborate goblets made at Nuremberg. They were very elaborate vessels with multi-knopped stems which were the glass counterparts of the goblets made by the Nuremberg goldsmiths in the 16th and 17th centuries. They look as if they were made for show rather than for use.

By the early 18th century the use of a new and improved metal which had originated in Bohemia spread to Germany, particularly in the districts of Silesia and Saxony. This was a lime-potash glass which was very clear and hard. It lent itself to cutting and engraving, so covered goblets with knopped and faceted stems became popular. This skill was brought to Germany by the engravers of Bohemia.

Some coloured glass was made in Germany, and the most important name connected with its development was that of Johann Kunckel, who was a chemist rather than a glassmaker. He worked in Potsdam and produced various colours of fine glass. He is thought to have used gold as the colouring agent for his red glass instead of the more usual copper.

Right *A German flask elaborately engraved by Anton Mauerl of Nuremberg, and dated 1719.*

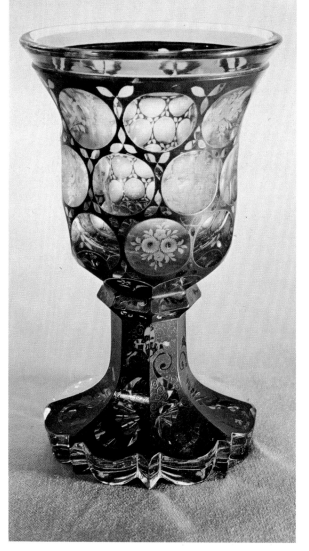

Bohemia

BOHEMIA, that part of the Habsburg lands which became integrated with Czecho-slovakia after the First World War, is another of those areas of Europe which established an identity and a reputation for itself strong enough for the name still to mean something to most people today. Records of glassmaking date from the 14th century, and because of the abundant supplies of wood for fuel and the raw materials for the glass, the craft soon established itself. There were many families who created the tradition, and one of them, the Schurer family, continued in the trade for nearly 300 years, from 1540 to the early 18th century. Glassmaking became such an important part of the industrial life of Bohemia that by the end of the 19th century Hartshorne states that there were fifty-six glasshouses operating.

Bohemian glass started to acquire its individual character in the late 16th century with the introduction of cutting and engraving. *Façon de Venise* had spread northwards through Europe, and among the techniques that came with it was the art of cutting glass as if it were rock crystal. This style caught the imagination of the Bohemian glassworkers, and Caspar Lehmann is credited with being the first important native worker to adopt the technique. It was from this beginning that the great Bohemian tradition of cutting and engraving arose.

In the early 17th century another innovation by the Bohemians combined with their skill in engraving to produce some of the most remarkable examples of this technique ever seen. This was the development of a new metal which required the addition of lime to the potash-silica mixture then being used. The result was a hard clear glass which retained its

Opposite top right *A German 18th-century tumbler decorated in the* Zwischengold-glas *technique. This consists of transparent enamel and gilt decoration sealed between two layers of glass. It was a revival of the technique used in Rome during the 1st century.*

Opposite bottom right *An elaborate Bohemian overlay goblet of the 19th century. The main part of the glass is overlaid with black and amber, but the floral reserves which are cut through are themselves overlaid in different colours.*

Opposite far left *A covered goblet decorated in* Schwarz-lot *by Abraham Helmback, and made about 1690. This technique, although apparently plain, permitted great delicacy and detail.*

Left *A superb Bohemian beaker of the 19th century, gilded and enamelled, with diamond cutting round the base.*

clarity even when thick-walled vessels were made. Not only did this new metal produce more attractive vessels, but it enabled the engraver to indulge in deeper and more impressive engraving. Political troubles in the early 17th century led to the dispersal of the engravers throughout Germany, where engraving became a popular method of decorating glass. It is true to say, however, that it was in Bohemia that the finest work of this kind was carried out. Towards the end of the 17th century the taste for *Façon de Venise* declined, and was replaced by a new style which made use of the qualities of the improved metal. Goblets with round funnel bowls had knopped stems cut with facets, well proportioned but less ornate than the Venetian equivalent. The glass was thicker and the bowls were often cut with vertical panels and had domed covers to match. The bowl, the cover and sometimes even the foot would be profusely covered with highly ornate baroque decoration interrupted by coats of arms or formal scenes. Later, in the 18th and during the 19th century, more naturalistic themes were introduced, which included woodland scenes with deer.

So highly was this combination of glass and engraving regarded that Bohemian artists were persuaded to go to Venice and Spain to introduce the techniques there.

Although cutting and engraving were among the most important of the decorative arts to be developed in Bohemia, several other techniques well known to antiquity were revived by Bohemian glassmakers and given a distinctive quality which makes them much sought after by collectors today. About 1725 the art of enclosing a pattern of gold leaf and transparent enamel between two layers of glass was revived. This technique originated in Italy in the early years of the Christian era (see page 11). The inner layer of glass had a lip on the outer surface on to which the outer layer butted, thus making a close fitting joint which completely protected the delicate film of incised gold leaf inside.

At about the same period Ignatius Preissler was establishing a reputation for his painting on glass. His usual subjects were *chinoiserie* scenes enclosed in baroque scrolls painted in black enamel, and frequently highlighted with gold.

In the early 19th century the black basalt wares of the Wedgwood factory were very popular, and this taste was reflected in black glass vessels made in Bohemia. Dating from 1822 it was called Hyalith, and one of the

A very fine Bohemian goblet, signed C. Hillé, with red overlay which is heavily cut through to reveal a hunting scene on the bowl. The stem and foot are cut with facets. This was a style of engraving at which Bohemian artists excelled. On the opposite page we see a detail of the deep carving.

best-known makers was Frederick Egermann. He was an enterprising man who was responsible for a number of new varieties of glassware. In addition to the Hyalith he also made glass to imitate natural stone such as agate, jasper and marble.

Egermann also experimented with coloured glass using chemicals that preserved the transparency of the glass. Opaque white glass was also well known, and in the early 19th century these two were combined to produce the overlay glass whose popularity lasted throughout the 19th century. It usually consists of a layer of white glass over a base of transparent green, red or blue glass. The white is then cut through to show "windows" of the coloured glass underneath. The whole was then decorated with gilding or coloured enamel. The idea was taken one step further later in the century when the overlay was reduced to one or two medallions. These were decorated in coloured enamel with portraits, usually of young ladies, or with bunches of flowers, while the body of the vessel was covered with a fine meandering pattern in gilt. This style of ware was usually made as ornamental ewers or vases.

A cheaper but effective method of producing coloured glass was to cover the outside of a clear glass vessel with a film of coloured glass. This was applied either as a stain or by dipping in a pot of the desired colour. The commonest colours are a rich yellow–produced with uranium–and red, but green and amethyst also occur. Some glasses cut with vertical panels have each panel coated with a different colour. If the vessel was embellished with engraved decoration the thin layer of colour was easily removed to show the clear glass underneath. Popular subjects were views of spa towns on beakers and tumblers which were sold as souvenirs. Although they were probably not very expensive when they were made, the engraving is always of a high standard.

In the late 19th century when the Art Nouveau movement was getting under way, a Viennese, Louis Lobmeyr, started a factory to produce glass of a high artistic and technical quality using Bohemian craftsmen. This was a reaction against the vast quantities of cheaply made mass-produced glassware which was made everywhere during the second half of the 19th century. This effort to revive glassmaking as an art was continued by the Loetz glassworks where beautifully coloured iridescent glass was made.

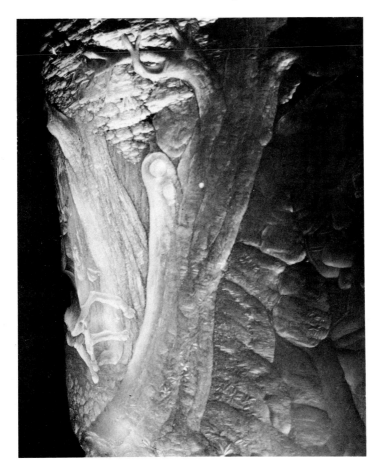

Above *The Loetz factory, although started by an Austrian, was staffed by Bohemian glassworkers. This example is typical of the iridescent effect achieved on this 19th-century art glass.*

Opposite *An amethyst serving bottle from the Low Countries. It is late 17th century, and a rarity, as coloured glass from this period is unusual.*

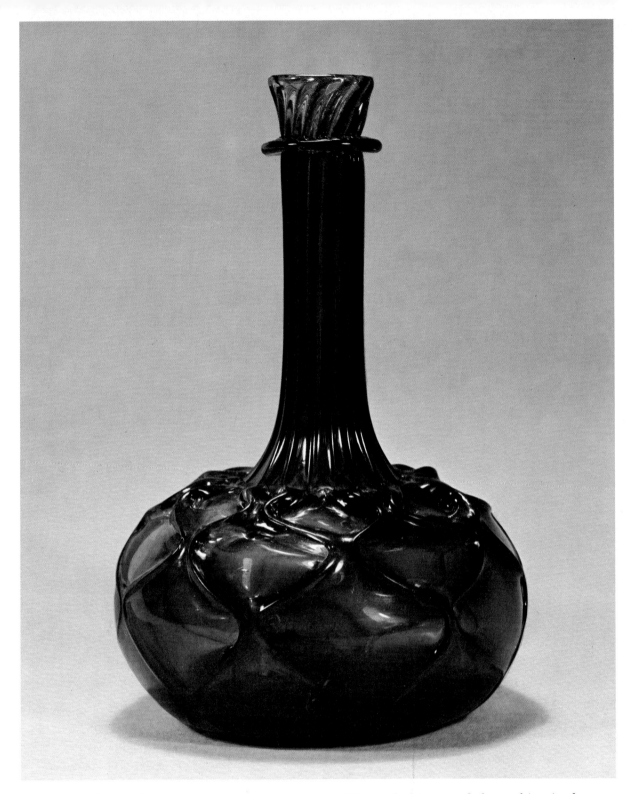

The Low Countries

THE last of the three northern European sections is even more difficult to define than the others. Geographically it comprised the area between the Rhine and Mosel rivers which now forms part of Germany, the seven provinces of the Netherlands and the general area of Belgium, including what are now parts of northern France. It was equally difficult to define politically as it was rarely all under one rule at any time and was variously controlled by the Spanish and the Austrians.

The early history of glassmaking in the area is as vague as that of the rest of northern Europe, and it first comes into prominence with the introduction of Venetian glass in the 15th century. The new Venetian *cristallo* which was such an improvement over its predecessors was displayed and advertised in all the courts of Europe, and seems particularly to have attracted attention in the Low Countries. There are records of glasshouses being established to make the *façon de Venise* in Antwerp in 1537, at Liège in 1569 and at Amsterdam in 1597. These houses employed both Venetian and Altarist glassmakers. The trade flourished, and the whole area became the most important in Europe outside Venice to produce glassware in the Venetian style. Its distance from Venice, however, led to slight differences in character, and it is a matter of considerable difficulty to distinguish the glass made in the local glassworks from that imported from Venice.

While the *façon de Venise* flourished other glassworks in the principal towns as well as many others in minor centres continued to turn out masses of utilitarian wares in the traditional styles of the region. This local tradition still made use of the *Waldglas* which has been mentioned earlier, but by the 16th and 17th centuries it had developed into a metal that effected a whole range of blue-greens.

The *Roemer* was one of the native styles which acquired great popularity, and several types, identified by the prunts applied to the stems, have been particularly identified with the Low Countries. One of these employed prunts which were flattened and smoothed to the point where they blended into the wall of the vessel. This produced different depths of colour according to the varying thickness of glass. Two other prunt variations were those moulded on the surface with a face of Neptune and those with beads of blue glass applied to the centres. These last two seem to me to be a direct result of the *façon de Venise* influence.

During the 17th century *Roemer* stands were made. They were tall pedestals in precious metals designed to have a *Roemer* clamped into a mounting on the top. Due to the proportions of the *Roemers* then in use this had the effect of producing a tall metal goblet with a glass bowl. The total effect was reminiscent of the elaborate tall goblets made by the Nuremberg goldsmiths.

Another style peculiar to the Low Countries was the tall narrow flute. This was a very thinly blown glass up to 18 inches high and about 2 inches wide. The funnel bowl was usually mounted onto a single hollow knop and a spreading foot. Very few of these fragile glasses have survived to the present day.

At the end of the 17th century the new styles of glass being made in England and Bohemia started to gain favour throughout Europe, and the Venetian style went into a decline. The Bohemian glassmakers had an efficient marketing organization and set up warehouses in the Netherlands to stock their products. English lead glass was also popular and during the 18th century the English styles were much imitated by local glasshouses.

The traffic was not all one way, however. Elaborate baskets and dessert services were made in Liège during the late 17th and early 18th centuries which were popular in England, as newspaper advertisements of the period show. These vessels were made of threads of glass built up in layers to produce an open-mesh pattern. They stood on glass plates decorated with a border executed in the same style.

Under the heading of Low Countries it now only remains to consider the work of the Dutch engravers. Engraving was the only one of the applied methods of decorating glass which achieved any degree of importance in the Low Countries, and throughout the 17th and 18th centuries there were a number of artists whose work was of the highest order. The technique as developed in Holland was quite different from that practised in Bohemia. Dutch engraving was carried out on the surface of the vessel with the delicacy of painting, while Bohemian engraving depended on a good thickness of metal and was more closely allied to sculpture.

One of the earliest of the recorded Dutch engravers was Anna Roemers Visscher, who was one of the very few women known to have been engaged in this work. There exists an engraved *Roemer* bearing her signature and the date 1643. She specialized in a free-flowing style of calligraphic engraving, a method also favoured by Willem van Heemskerk in the 17th century and by Hendrik Scholting in the 18th.

Opposite left *A 16th-century goblet from the Netherlands with a blow-moulded bowl and stem. The thistle-shaped bowl has applied prunts and medallions, and the hollow stem has lions' heads moulded on it.*

Below left *A Netherlands flute glass of the late 17th century. The tall narrow bowl is engraved with foliage and a portrait of William of Orange. The short stem consists of a hollow inverted baluster.*

Below *A stipple-engraved wine glass signed J. van den Blyk. This most difficult of all engraving techniques. (see p. 64) found its most skilled exponents in Holland during the 18th century.*

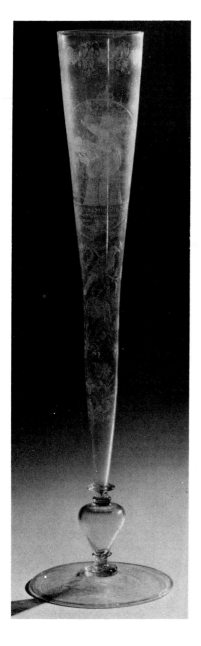

The 18th century saw the finest work being produced by artists such as Frans Greenwood, David Wolff and Jacob Sang, whose names must be known to all collectors of old glass. The first two specialized in stipple engraving. This is a method whereby the surface of the glass is broken by repeated light blows with a diamond-pointed tool. The density of the marks thus produced determines the variations in tone and shading of the finished picture. The resulting effect is rather like that of a thin photographic negative. It requires a complete sureness of touch and considerable artistic ability for its success. Because of these demands on the artist it was never widely practised, but there are today a few engravers working in England who can produce stippled decoration comparable in quality to that of the 18th-century Dutch masters.

Jacob Sang specialized in wheel engraving, and his work has a delicacy, precision and sureness of touch which few people have ever equalled. Foremost among his works are those glasses which he engraved with coats of arms. The glasses most popular with the 18th-century Dutch engravers were English lead glasses, particularly those of the Newcastle light baluster style.

While much of Low Countries' glassmaking took its inspiration from other sources, its engravers created a standard against which all others must be compared.

A Dutch-made façon de Venise *wine glass of the 17th century. The hexagonal bowl is set on an elaborate serpentine stem decorated with pincered blue trailing. The style is subtly different from the same thing made in Venice.*

A Dutch Roemer *of the 17th century with a wide bowl decorated with a band of sailing ships in the* Schwarzlot *technique. The stem has prunts which have been smoothed in until they nearly meet.*

England after 1850

TOWARDS the middle of the 19th century
the orderly progression from one style to
another which had occurred during the pre-
vious 150 years collapsed. Influences from
abroad, notably Bohemia, had a marked effect
on design in England, and the introduction of
new production techniques such as press
moulding from America led to cheaper glassware catering for a much wider market than
ever before. National and international exhibitions culminating in the Great Exhibition
of 1851 introduced many new styles to the
British public. It is appropriate to this narrative
that the building, erected especially for the
purpose, in which the Exhibition was held was
the Crystal Palace, an enormous structure
completely sheathed in glass. One of its
principal features was a glass fountain weighing
about four tons, built by the firm of T. & C.
Osler of Birmingham.

At the exhibition were shown all the finest
designs and newest manufacturing methods
from all parts of the world. When it was over
glassmaking in England changed radically:
as the Industrial Revolution gathered momen-
tum and manufacturing units became larger,
small firms using traditional hand methods
became uneconomic. This led to the concen-
tration of the glass industry into fewer
companies, and glassmaking declined in areas
like Bristol and London. It settled principally
on the areas around Stourbridge and Birmingham (only ten miles apart) and on the rivers
Tyne and Wear around Newcastle where there
was an abundance of fuel and raw materials.

Whereas in earlier years every glassmaker
had been content to produce what was in
popular demand, after 1851 each manufacturer endeavoured to produce designs quite
different from those of his competitors. To
protect their interests designs were registered,
and during the second half of the century
literally thousands of patterns for glassware
were registered. The changes in style and taste
were so rapid that it becomes much more
difficult to date glass after 1850, but attribution,
on the grounds of style, to particular factories
is often easier. This is assisted by the practice
at some factories of marking the products with
the name of the company. The taste for
Continental glass was encouraged by the
Great Exhibition, and Bohemian styles of
coloured and overlay glass as well as the French
style of opal and frosted glass decorated with
coloured glass buttons, became very popular.

*A cameo vase by Thomas Webb and Son, late
19th century. The white overlay is cut away in a
pattern of chrysanthemums. A similarity to the
Chinese example on page 33 can be seen, but the
English cameo work is much more subtle.*

Glass had to be made to suit all pockets so that there was a demand for high quality products for the wealthy as well as mass-produced wares for the working classes. This led to different techniques being adopted to produce the same style. A good example of this is the difference in quality that occurs in Bohemian style ruby glass. At one end of the scale this was made by covering a clear glass vessel with a layer of red glass. Expert workmen would then cut through the outer layer to expose panels of clear glass; at the other end cheap clear glass was first cut with facets and the surrounding areas were then filled in with a ruby stain. To produce the former foreign craftsmen were often brought to England to work in their own tradition while the cheaper versions could be made with almost any class of labour. Among the immigrant glassworkers who settled in Stourbridge were several decorators who established high reputations for their skill. Frederick Kny, William Fritsche and Paul Oppitz all executed the most beautiful engraving in the Bohemian tradition, and their work was shown at many exhibitions. Jules Barbe was a gilder in the French style whose work has never been bettered in this country.

All these craftsmen worked at one time or another for Thomas Webb & Son. Webb's, which was founded in 1856 and is still operating, is one of several firms which established the high reputation of Stourbridge glass in the 19th century. Others were Richardsons, Stevens & Williams and Boulton & Mills. In Birmingham George Bacchus & Sons, Rice Harris & Sons and T. & C. Osler were well known.

Opposite *Jug and tumbler, made by Richardson in the mid–19th century. This is part of a water set in clear glass enamelled in green and yellow with irises.*

Below *An extremely fine cameo vase of about 1900, signed by George Woodall, one of the best-known workers in this style. The delicacy of the shading almost looks painted.*

Opposite *A three-branched candlestick made in a naturalistic style to imitate tree branches. The glass is called Vaseline glass because of its oily yellow appearance.*

Below *A selection of wine glasses of the late 19th century illustrating various decorative techniques including coloured glass, overlay, staining and enamelling.*

Below *A goblet made about 1850 by J. Varnish & Co. of London. This is double-walled glass silvered on the outside, like the liners of vacuum flasks, covered with a layer of translucent blue glass which is cut away in panels. Like many Victorian objects the taste is doubtful but the quality is good.*

Left *A two-handled goblet made in Stourbridge in the late 19th century and gilded by Jules Barbe. The heavy encrustation of gold is typical of the French style of gilding, and the execution of this example is superb.*

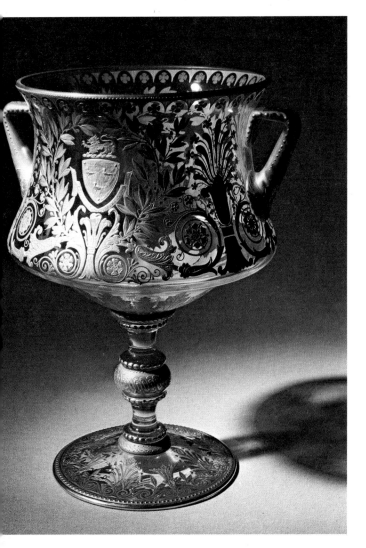

The English glassmakers did not take their ideas solely from European sources. In 1885 Queen Victoria received a gift of some Burmese glass which had just been invented at the Mount Washington Glass factory in America. She was very impressed by it and in a short while Thomas Webb & Son had agreed to make it under licence in England. This unusual glass shaded from pink to yellow, an effect which was achieved by the addition of gold and uranium to its ingredients.

Cameo glass was developed by John Northcote, a famous Stourbridge glassmaker, who was associated with the firm of Stevens & Williams. It was always very expensive as it required extreme skill and patience on the part of the carver. One of the best known of the decorators in this field was George Woodall, who worked for Thomas Webb & Son. He specialised in classical figures with flowing robes, and signed pieces of his work command very high prices today. Like everything else it had its imitators, and various methods were invented to produce glass that had the appearance of cameo work but which could be mass produced.

Although glassmaking largely died out in London the oldest glassmaking firm in the country is a London company, J. Powell & Sons, who were established about 1700. They made glass for William Morris, and have been responsible for fine handmade glassware in this century.

The other main centre of glassmaking in the 19th century was in the north of England. The area around Newcastle-on-Tyne was responsible for much of the cheap pressed glass made for the mass market. The technique was developed to a very high standard, and a glance through the catalogues of the Sowerby Glass Co. will show what a wide variety of goods was produced by this method. The most sought-after of this pressed glass today is slag glass. This was opaque glass in a variety of

A collection of "friggers" made in Stourbridge during the 19th century. Friggers were novelties which the glassmakers produced for their own amusement. Illustrated here are an umbrella, a water-pump and bucket, a mouse on a model of a glass pot (the clay vessel in which the molten glass was contained) and a pair of bellows. Larger objects like walking sticks, swords and trumpets made of glass were often carried when the Glass Makers Guild walked in procession.

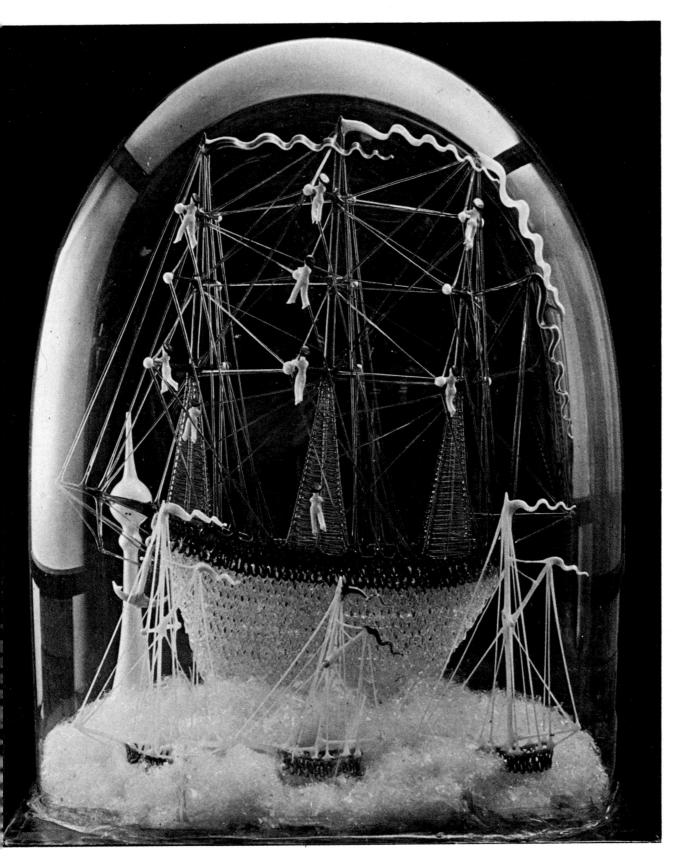

A sailing ship made entirely of glass with a lighthouse and three smaller vessels. These flights of fancy which demonstrated the glass-maker's manipulative skill were very popular during the 19th century.

colours the most typical of which has a purple and white marbled effect. The moulds in which it was made were works of art. The three most important companies which made slag glass, and who often added their trade mark to the moulds so that their products can be identified, were Sowerbys Ellison Glass Works, G. Davidson & Co. and H. Greener & Co.

As well as this moulded glass much coloured decorative glass was made in the north. It derived from the Venetian tradition with its liberal use of applied glass decoration. Baskets, spill vases and candlesticks were popular.

In the 20th century several attempts have been made to establish artist-craftsman studios in an attempt to break away from the mass production methods of the large factories. Among the better known of these are the names Greystan and Monart.

France

TO the student of glass the history of its progress and development in France presents a vague and uncertain picture. Under Roman rule it was a well colonized and cultured country and glassmaking was widespread. Its manufacture continued in all parts apparently without serious interruption, but a lack of strong national style and technical innovation meant that French glass never found much favour abroad or exercised any influence over other glassmaking centres in the way that Venetian or Bohemian glass did.

Early glass made in France is usually termed *verre de fougère* (fern glass) because the potash used in its manufacture was derived from the ashes of fern and bracken.

From earliest times French glassmakers acquired a widespread reputation for the manufacture of window glass, and documents dating from the 8th century include requests for their assistance in supplying the glazing for churches and monasteries in England. Many of the earliest stained-glass windows in English churches, dating from the 14th century, are of French origin. They were made from what is known as broad glass. That is, a large-diameter blown tube with the ends cut off and slit along its length. This was then heated so that the tube opened out into a flat sheet. This same process was also used to make mirror glass, but at the end of the 17th century Louis de Nehou invented the casting method to produce larger sheets of a more consistent thickness.

Left *A small glass figurine representing Louis XIV made at Nevers in France in the late 17th century. These figures were made of coloured glass manipulated over a flame, and are today quite rare.*

Left *Not much early French glass survives, but the 17th-century barrel and jug are typical of the decorative wares of the period. The effect is achieved by rolling chips of coloured glass into the still soft walls of a vessel which is being blown. These chips melt and can be rolled in on a marver plate to give the splattered effect.*

Below *Examples of French* millefiori *paperweights, made about 1850. The technique dates from Roman times, but the French glassmakers brought it to a high degree of perfection. The weights illustrated represent the work of the three leading firms, namely from left to right: Baccarat, Clichy and St Louis.*

Much domestic and tableware was made at all times in France, and during the 15th to 17th centuries the industry was very much influenced by the Venetian style – the large number of Italian names featuring in contemporary records show the extent to which Italian craftsmen were employed throughout France. None of these domestic wares seems to have been distinctive, and very few examples of the glass vessels made during these years have endured until the present. Well known, however, are small figurines in glass made during the 17th century at Nevers. They are made of opaque coloured glass.

It was not until the late 18th century that French glassmaking began to establish a reputation and identity of its own. In 1765 the forerunner of the Baccarat glassworks was founded, and in 1767 the St Louis factory was started nearby. Their reputations were built on a very fine quality glass, and since 1780, when the English style of lead crystal was introduced, the name Baccarat has always been associated with superb crystal glass. Much of it is distinguished by cut panels and flutes, with the feet of drinking glasses hexagonal in shape.

Another speciality was the enclosure of coloured medallions in the thickness of the glass.

About the middle of the 19th century the name became associated with the manufacture of glass paperweights. Although the idea originated in Venice, it was the French factories of Baccarat, St Louis and Clichy, with their variety and quality, which made them famous. The commonest style contains short sections of *millefiori* canes arranged in a pattern and set in glass, an idea which originated with the mosaic glass of pre-Roman times. The French makers soon developed the theme so that their paperweights enclosed glass models of flowers, fruit, vegetables, insects and reptiles. A number of them include dated canes for the years 1846–1849.

In the later years of the 19th century a tradition for "art" glass arose in France, and one of the leaders of this movement was Emil Gallé (1845–1904). During the 1870s he developed a distinctive style of cameo glass based on the Chinese taste. The shapes were elegant and the layers of pastel-coloured translucent glass were cut through usually to depict flowers, plants and natural scenes.

Opposite far left *A 16th-century goblet made in France in the façon de Venise, with a wide tapered bowl on a hollow stem and high foot. It is decorated in coloured enamels, and bears an inscription in French.*

Opposite middle *A French water jug of the 18th century. It is typical of the mass of good but undistinguished table glass that was produced in France over a very long period.*

Left *A 19th-century decanter and a wine glass from a service by Baccarat. Both the quality of the glass and the depth of cutting are typical of the work of this factory. Both items have a medallion showing a coat-of-arms set into the thickness of the wall.*

Below *A decorative bowl made at the factory of Réne Lalique in the early 20th century. It is moulded in high relief with a band of children and flowing draperies and has a "frosted" surface finish.*

About the turn of the 20th century René Lalique was the originator of a range of glass produced by casting and moulding, which relied largely on surface texture for its appeal. Important among his designs were vessels decorated in relief with fishes, birds and female figures in the Art Nouveau style.

Although it took many centuries to establish a reputation for imaginative domestic glassware, the products of 19th- and 20th-century France have found eager imitators.

Opposite top *An American early-19th-century blow-moulded decanter with three applied, milled neck rings.* Opposite below *The Tiffany Studios in New York produced some beautiful art glass, and this Favrile vase of about 1896 demonstrates their use of natural shapes and iridescent effect.*

Below *A vase made in the Syrian style by Emil Gallé, the manufacturer of art glass in France.*

America

GLASSMAKING came to America with the European settlers, and for two centuries the glass made there reflected the origins of its manufacturers. In the 19th century, however, as America became an industrial society, technical innovation led to the development of manufacturing techniques which Europe was only too glad to copy. The most important of these, connected with the glass trade, was the development of press moulding.

The first recorded glassworks was founded at Jamestown, Virginia, in 1608, although it is thought that the Spaniards may have introduced glassmaking to the west coast much earlier. For more than 100 years glassmaking continued in a haphazard manner, turning out domestic utensils of no great character or importance. The first glasshouse to establish a reputation and about which any detail is known was the Wistarberg glassworks in Salem County, New Jersey, started in 1739 by a buttonmaker named Wistar (1696–1752). Later, in 1763, William Henry Stiegel (1729–1785) experimented with glass and started the Stiegel glassworks at Manheim, Pennsylvania. He imported his workers from Europe, and 18th-century glassware was made in the English and German styles. The most difficult problem now is to distinguish locally made glassware from imported articles.

The Syrian glassmakers of the early Christian era had been masters at the art of blow moulding. That is the free blowing of glass into open moulds. These might be one piece if the vessel to be blown tapered inwards to the base so that it could easily be extracted from the mould, or two piece if there were diameters to be blown which were larger than the neck. The American glass blowers adopted this technique and used it for a variety of wares such as flasks and bottles. The moulded decoration was often of a commemorative nature, and particularly well known among these are coloured bottles bearing the legends "Union" and "Liberty".

In the early 19th century the even older technique of moulding in a closed mould was revived and improved by the process of press moulding. By this method flat or tapered vessels were formed in a two-piece mould; one half being used to compress the slug of molten glass into the shape of the other half so that at the point where the two halves met the mould was full. With this method far more intricate patterns could be produced with much sharper definition, and perhaps even more important, articles could be produced at a faster rate.

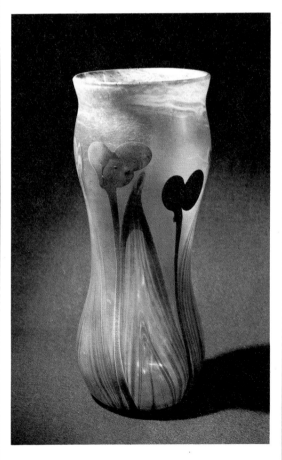

The earliest recorded patent for this process was taken out in 1829 when presses were manually operated. During the next fifty years a whole succession of patents was taken out covering both improvements in power presses and moulding processes whereby several articles could be moulded at one time. This process enabled a wide variety of glassware to be made at prices which put cheap copies of cut and decorative glass into every home.

In the context of this exchange of ideas and techniques between the old world and the new it is interesting to note that Harry Northwood, son of one of the greatest of the Stourbridge glassmakers, John Northwood, emigrated to America in 1885, and three years later was running his own glassworks.

As well as the production of utilitarian wares, the continuing search for novelty culminated in a wide variety of flasks and bottles made to represent everything imagin-able: people, animals, birds, fruit, buildings and railway engines, to name but a few.

Towards the end of the 19th century, American glassmakers became involved in the Art Nouveau movement, and much elegant and decorative glass was made. The most famous figure was probably Louis Comfort Tiffany (1848–1933), who had a studio in New York, where he produced a whole variety of imaginative coloured glass whose chief attraction was its iridescence. One of his largest undertakings was the remarkable glass curtain for the stage of the National Theatre of Mexico, the Bellas Artes, in Mexico City.

In more recent years glass artists working for such companies as the Steuben Glass Co. have created individual works which explore to the full the possibilities of shape and decoration, and which show that man is still intrigued by a material that has inspired his forebears for more than 3500 years.

Two late-18th-century American blow-moulded bottles. The left-hand one commemorates the union of the States and includes a masonic emblem. The right-hand one is a bottle advertising the Huffsey Glass works.

Above *A superb example of the modern trend for artists to explore the possibilities of glass. This piece, called Zephyr, produced in 1950 for the Steuben Glass Co. of Corning, New York, combines form and decoration to give a strong impression of movement. It is almost as if the glass were still plastic. The glass itself was designed by George Thompson, and the engraving by Don Wier.*

Top *An American 19th-century glass tray in pressed lace glass commemorating the American warship* Constitution. *It was quite a difficult technical feat to fill a wide shallow mould like this and achieve good definitions over the whole surface.*

This double-gourd-shaped vase by Tiffany illustrates an iridescent effect which was popular among the art glassmakers of the late 19th century.